The Philosophy of Narayana Guru

The Philosophy of Narayana Guru

Swami Muni Narayana Prasad

DK PRINTWORLD
Publishers of Indian Traditions

Cataloging in Publication Data — DK
[Courtesy: D.K. Agencies (P) Ltd. <docinfo@dkagencies.com>]

Narayana Prasad, *Muni,* 1938- **author.**

The philosophy of Narayana Guru / Swami Muni Narayana Prasad. – Third impression.

pages cm

Includes bibliographical references and index.

ISBN 9788124602362 (PB)

1. Narayana Guru, 1856-1928. 2. Hindu philosophy. 3. Vedanta. I. Title.

BL1175.N38N37 2017 DDC 181.4 23

ISBN 13: 978-81-246-0236-2 (PB)

First Published in India in 2003
Second impression in 2010
Third impression in 2017

Printed and published by :
D.K. Printworld (P) Ltd.
Regd. office : *Vedaśrī*, F-395, Sudarshan Park
ESI Metro Station, New Delhi - 110 015
Phones : (011) 2545 3975, 2546 6019
e-mail : indology@dkprintworld.com
Web : www.dkprintworld.com

"As with waves in ocean, individuated entities, one after another, do emerge and merge back. Lo and behold, this does not end! It is just the ceaseless *karma* that inheres in the primeval ocean of *samvit* (Consciousness)."

(*Ātmopadeśa Śatakam* of Narayana Guru, Verse, 56)

PREFACE

THE Board of Studies of the Mahatma Gandhi University in the Kerala State of India once mooted the idea of introducing the Philosophy of Narayana Guru in its Faculty of Philosophy. But the idea had to be dropped for the reason that no proper book worth using as a textbook was available then on the subject. We in the Narayana Gurukula felt that this lack had to be rectified, and the present book is its outcome.

Academic studies on Vedānta, in the normal course, follow a path much different from the one followed by seekers guided by traditional *gurus*. What the universities are interested in with respect to Vedānta, as with all other subjects, is the academic correctness of thinking. The method they follow is logical reasoning, which in its turn depends on the law of causality. The extent to which causality is an unquestionable law is a bone of contention amongst academics themselves. The interest of and method relied on by traditional masters are much different. A master is a person who has realised the ultimate meaning of life, making actual life free of all bondages and entanglements. The goal of the seekers who approach such masters is attaining this realisation. Logical reasoning alone is not the only method they resort to. Such reasoning is possible only with regard to things or phenomena observed in nature. The meaning content of the observer or the seeker's own self is never observable, and to that extent is not amenable to logical reasoning. It therefore requires a new method of reasoning, if at all this method could be considered 'reasoning'. Such a method has always been resorted to by all masters all over the world, some consciously and some unconsciously. We, in the present book, have tried our best to clarify this method. Still the students and professors alike may find it difficult to follow it, simply because it is something quite unfamiliar to them. Yet we plead that the philosophy of Narayana Guru, and for that matter the philosophy of any great master, will not yield itself to the students without recourse to this time-honoured method. Academics, in other words, will have to accommodate themselves to this line of thought if their intention is imbibing the real spirit of the philosophy of Narayana Guru.

The developent of thought in the present book follows almost that of the *Ātmopadeśa Śatakam* (One Hundred Verses of Self-Instruction) of the Guru, with the exception that the sections dealing with Ethics, Religion and Aesthetics have been pulled out to be included in Part II of the book. The other chapters that find place in Part II are on Casteism, and God, Temples and Rites. The former is a social phenomenon the Guru fought against vehemently but not violently. And for this reason it so happened that the Guru was dubbed as a social reformer, completely unmindful of the original contributions he made to Indian Philosophy and to philosophy in general. Part I of the book deals with pure philosophy.

Many relevant sidelights have been left just hinted at, for the sake of brevity of the book. Those who are interested in all such details are advised to read the present author's commentaries on the *Vedānta Sūtras* of Narayana Guru, as well as on the Upaniṣads and the *Bhagavad Gītā. Basic Lessons on India's Wisdom, Karma and Reincarnation* and *Vedānta up to Narayana Guru,* again by the same author, are also recommanded.

Dr. Peter Oppenheimer of U.S.A., a long time Gurukula friend, has been kind enough to go through the entire text, editing it and helping to clarify certain points that were felt to be not quite clear. Our indebtedness to him is not something personal, but is part of the indebtedness to the Absolute, which in effect is no indebtedness at all. So is our gratitude to Messrs. D. K. Printworld of New Delhi who have always been willing to publish all the serious studies of ours on Indian Philosophy.

This book, meant though for universities, we hope, would be of much help for those who are interested in the Philosophy of

Narayana Guru in particular and Advaita Vedānta in general as well as in rediscovering the spirit of the ancient wisdom of India in the Age of Science.

It is the discipleship of the present writer under Nataraja Guru and Guru Nitya Chaitanya Yati that enabled him to condense the philosophy of Narayana Guru in this small book. And, it was Nataraja Guru himself who helped unlock the above-mentioned other-than-logical reasoning. With prostrations at the feet of the original Guru, Narayana Guru, and my direct *gurus*, Nataraja Guru and Nitya Chaitanya Yati, this disciple offers this book for serious consideration to academics and wisdom lovers alike.

Varkala
February 10, 2003

Swami Muni Narayana Prasad

INTRODUCTION

IF any philosophy is to be worth the time it takes to examine it, the end result must be to reward its adherent in some appreciable way. Philosophy holds out the promise of a whole range of human values including clarity, comfort, calm, seeing the humour in otherwise troubling situations, understanding the laws that govern our emotions and fortunes, happiness, harmony, inner peace and in some rare cases even spiritual bliss. Just as a tree is to be known by its fruit and the testing of a pudding is in the eating, a philosophy can be evaluated by the degree to which it is capable of improving one's life experience. By this measure the Philosophy of Narayana Guru is to be acknowledged as a treasure for all humankind.

In my own case, I had the advantage of sampling the fruit even before perceiving the tree. Flash back 30 years to my first visit to India. As a young man, recently graduated from one of the most prestigious universities in the United States, I was undergoing something of a severe identity crisis. Having spent my entire life successfully learning how to excel in the role of student, I now felt ill-prepared for living life outside the confines of the artificial world of academia. If truth be told, I was totally fed up with philosophy itself, which at that point I considered to be little else besides vain, sterile hairsplitting and logic-chopping put forward by ineffectual men in 'ivory towers' that had little or no relation to the flesh and blood of actual day-to-day life. In fact, the underlying purpose of my travelling was to come into more direct contact with the heart and pulse of real life as opposed to abstracted life.

Through much misdirection and many an ill-conceived turn (too convoluted to present here but which is narrated in detail in my book *Mirror by the Road*), I unwittingly landed up at the front gate of the Narayana Gurukula in Varkala, South India. Both literally lost and at a loss, I was greeted and welcomed by a young man named Prasad. He took my hands in his in a gesture of warm welcome and asked me what I needed. Unable to even answer this seemingly simple question, I blurted out something to the effect of my wanting to learn Haṭha Yoga. With a gentle tone, he told me that Haṭha Yoga was not taught there, but that they did teach about Yoga in its broader sense such as is presented in the *Bhagavad Gītā*. At the time, that meant nothing to me. "Anyway", he said, "you look rather tired and you must be hungry and thirsty. Please come in and stay with us for some time. Whenever you feel refreshed and ready, you can continue your journey."

I was given a small cottage on a hillside at the back of the *āśrama* overlooking a sea of coconut palms up from which wafted the musical sounds of children playing and families praying. I was told when meal times were, and shown to a library of books in case I might like something to read. When I asked about payment, the question was brushed aside with the assurance that there was no charge for staying there. That itself was very remarkable and confusing to me.

As days turned into weeks, I was fascinated to observe that also no pressure was put on me to accept any particular religion or creed, and that my attendance at the Gurukula classes, chantings, 'prayer' sessions and periods of 'teamwork', whereby the buildings and grounds were maintained and developed, was as optional as were any monetary payments. All the people staying there, children and adults alike, seemed to be extraordinarily bright, friendly, patient and generous. They seemed to want nothing from me, but cared only about my well-being and happiness.

Now I was really intrigued. What made these people all so happy and caring? Certainly it was not material wealth, because by Western standards these people were 'poor'. No TV, no car, no cushy furniture, no bloated bank balance. For the first time in my life I wanted to know something about philosophy, specifically what kind of philosophy of life did these people hold dear that allowed them to be so cheerful and content, so attentive and undemanding. When I asked Prasad about this, he suggested that I read *The Word of the*

Guru (The Life and Teachings of Narayana Guru written by his disciple Nataraja Guru).

Thus began for me a long drawn love affair with Narayana Guru and his philosophy as conveyed to me primarily through my thirty year discipleship to Guru Nitya Chaitanya Yati and my association with the many inmates and supporters of the Narayana Gurukula Movement. During that period of time I also earned a Masters Degree in Psychology and a Doctorate in Education for which both my thesis and dissertation were directly based on the teachings of Narayana Guru, specifically his *Ātmopadeśa Śatakam* (One Hundred Verses of Self-Instruction). During these intervening years of studying the philosophy of Narayana Guru, my fascination has turned into adoration, and my questions have been converted into convictions. Significantly, these convictions do not lead me to contend with the convictions of others, but on the contrary make it possible for me to acknowledge and accommodate all points of view. Now, who was that Prasad who first welcomed me so warmly and then patiently waited until I was ready before introducing me to the Philosophy of Narayana Guru? He is one and the same Swami Muni Narayana Prasad who has written the present book, and in an ironic turning of the tables has asked me to introduce it to you.

Muni Prasad has devoted over four decades of his life to learning, living and interpreting the teaching of Narayana Guru, and in the present volume he encapsulates his search and discoveries in a very thorough and illuminating manner. In Part One of this volume we, the readers, are not only led to a greater understanding of a great man and his thought, but more importantly we are led to a greater vision and understanding of our own dear self. This vision is not simply of academic interest, but is capable of dramatically transforming our personal experience of self, other, the world, and life itself. In Part Two Muni Prasad presents the application of the philosophy in terms of ethics, aesthetics, and religious experience.

Narayana Guru was a thoroughgoing scientist in his approach to truth and at the same time a mystic and a poet in his vision and exposition. His philosophy was not expounded through lengthy discourses, but presented in pithy verses meant for singing and soaring high, for delving and diving deep. While singing in rapture, he somehow still managed to catalogue the powers and functions of the human mind, including the numerous types of errors to which it is prone, as well as detailing the inner discipline necessary to avoid or counteract those errors. His philosophy was at once descriptive and prescriptive. From the alpha depths of ontological truth to the omega heights of mystical vision and identity with the Absolute, all items of human interest, folly and aspiration find a place in his overall scheme, like so many pearls strung on a necklace.

His philosophy is basically a revaluation and restatement of Advaita Vedānta, which has been running like a cool, clarifying and nourishing stream throughout India's long and venerable history, but which by the time of Narayana Guru had gotten entangled in the polemics of its more pedantic advocates and marginalised as the private domain of an intellectual elite. The hallmark of the Guru's philosophy is indeed *advaita* (non-duality). He declares and illumines a union of self and other, more intimate than a lovers' embrace. His message is one of the unlimited creativity, freedom, bliss and immortality of the Self. He holds out for us the tantalising and well-considered conclusion that at its core the Self is universally and eternally of the nature of Being/Knowledge/Bliss. And, furthermore, if contemplated upon deeply, all the peripheral, specific and fleeting manifestations both within and around us can similarly be known and appreciated as ultimately non-different from this ever-elaborating core of the Self.

The philosophy of Narayana Guru is presented here in such a cogent and convincing manner that we are shown not only how all this can be so, but how it cannot but be so. It is with a sense of both gratitude and celebration that I commend this book to all seekers after truth, goodness and beauty. Ultimately, you will find that the sweet nectar-like taste, which you savour through the wonder and beauty of the Guru's global vision, is none other than the eternal yet ever-fresh flavour of your very own nature.

Kerala, India
February 2003

Dr. Peter Oppenheimer

CONTENTS

Part Two
Application

PART ONE
THE PHILOSOPHY

1

Preliminaries

'Love of Wisdom' — this is how philosophy is often defined. A loan-word, it derives from the Greek *philo* meaning 'loving', and *sophia* signifying 'wisdom'. Originally the Greek word *sophia* had a much wider range of application than the modern English word 'wisdom'. Wherever intelligence can be exercised in practical affairs, in mechanical arts, in business, there is room for *sophia*. Homer used it to refer to the skill of a carpenter. Moreover, modern English draws a fairly sharp distinction between the search for wisdom and the attempt to satisfy intellectual curiosity. Briefly, then, *philosophia* etymologically connotes the love of exercising one's curiosity and intelligence rather than the love of wisdom.[1]

This connotation has more or less remained unchanged, at least in the West, though each philosopher's attempt to satisfy his intellectual curiosity was always coloured by his own predilections. Thus, the common goal of all of them has been finding a body of reasoned-out answers to all the basic problems of life. This has remained true irrespective of their leanings towards either logic or mysticism.

Different is the case of philosophy in the East, especially in India. More than satisfying intellectual curiosity, ensuring happiness (*ānanda*) in life has always been the ultimate goal of Eastern philosophers. In other words, philosophy for them was a value-science.

---

1. Cf. *Encyclopedia of Philosophy*, Collier Macmillan, London, 1972 vols. 5 and 6, p. 216.

Yet another definition of philosophy is 'thinking about thinking'.[2] Our thinking supposedly is based on logical reason and association of ideas, both having perceptual knowledge for their basis. Thinking thus can be perception-based; but how can 'thinking about thinking' be so? Even empiricists (those who believe that all knowledge is derived from sense-experiences) will have to admit that such thinking necessarily has to be introspective or rather intuitive. The theory that all knowledge is derived from sense-experience, too, is not derived from sense-experience, but from intuition. Experiential intuitive perception being an attitude that goes well with the Eastern Philosophy, this second definition above can be considered as leaning towards the East rather than to the West. More related to religion than to philosophy proper is the apperceptive, introspective or rather intuitive vision known to the West. The break between the two (philosophy and religion), we know, was the result of the reaction against the nightmarish Inquisition. The aversion for religion fanned out as a sort of revolt amongst free thinkers against everything related to religion, and later it became deep-rooted in the culture of the Modern Age. The historical consequence relevant here is the separation of philosophy and religion, which till then, till the end of the Dark Ages, were inseparable. Having witnessed no Inquisition-like torments, the East, particularly India, still continues to treat philosophy and religion as inseparable. And therefore, Indian Philosophy virtually means Hindu Philosophy, Buddhist Philosophy and Jaina Philosophy together.

The word equivalent to 'philosophy' in India is *darśana*, meaning 'vision'. Vision of what? The vision of the Real, of what really exists. Each school of thought is called a *darśana*,[3] and aiming at the

---

2. *The Oxford Companion of Philosophy*, Oxford University Press, 1995, p. 666.

3. Twelve such schools of thought are traditionally recognised in India: Six of them orthodox schools (*āstika darśanas*) and six others heterodox schools (*nāstika darśanas*). The former six are Nyāya, Vaiśeṣika, Sāṅkhya, Yoga, Pūrva-Mīmāṁsā and Uttara-Mīmāṁsā; the latter six are the Cārvākas (Indian materialists), Jainism and the four Buddhist Schools (Sautrāntika, Vaibhāṣika, Yogācāra, Mādhyamika).

happiness of everyone, individually and collectively, is common among all of them. In other words, how can happiness in life be ensured by knowing the Reality that appears as life, is the central theme of all Indian schools of thought.

Vedānta, particularly Advaita Vedānta, admittedly represents the finality of Indian wisdom, as the very word suggests: 'Vedānta' literally meaning 'the finality' (*anta*) of knowledge (*veda*). In the sense that it is the body of wisdom contained in the Upaniṣads, the concluding section (*anta*) of the Vedas, also it is called 'Vedānta'. Originally the Upaniṣads were themselves called Vedāntas. The Upaniṣadic wisdom as interpreted by the great Śaṅkara is known as Advaita Vedānta, meaning non-dualistic Vedānta. Śaṅkara expounded the hidden wisdom of the Upaniṣads (*upaniṣad* means 'hidden wisdom') in the eighth century AD fully in line with the scientific preciseness and rational integrity familiar then. Re-introducing the same wisdom in the modern Age of Science, giving full recognition to the scientific mindset of the days in which he lived, was what Narayana Guru did. Exemplifying how non-dualism, as an applied wisdom, enhances the value of human life and human dignity in both the individual and social dimensions, is the crowning touch the Guru gave to this wisdom of antiquity.

The Problems

Philosophy, both Eastern and Western, always attempts to answer two basic questions: 'Who am I?', and 'From where and how did this world come into being?'[4] Any answer to these questions, to be comprehensive and convincing, will have to take into account and correlate three basic factors of existence: my own existence as the knower, the existence of the world I encounter and know, and the unknown and unknowable that we are compelled to admit the existence of. Should the last mentioned be given a legitimate place in philosophy? Yes, because even our most scientifically conceived enquiry, whether at the quantum level of sub-atomic existence or at the astro-physical level of the ever-expanding universe, lands us in

4. See Verse 1 of *Brahmavidyā Pañcakam* (*Brahmavidyā* in Five Verses) of Narayana Guru.

some inexplicable mystery. Admitting mystery into the realm of philosophy proper is not anathema to Indian Philosophy, though this is not the case in the West.

I, the knower, the subject, am an inseparable part of the mysterious whole, and therefore knowing who I really am means knowing the reality that underlies the world. Furthermore, knowing the causal reality of the world means knowing what is real in me.

A definite answer to the first question 'Who am I?', therefore, implies a definite answer to the second, 'From where and how did this world come into being?' as well. In other words, a genuine attempt to answer either of the questions answers the other as well.

The word 'world' (*loka*, *prapañca* or *jagat*) here signifies more than the earth; it includes within its scope the entire cosmic system and the life in it, where mind and matter remain undivided. Put in the traditional mythological terms familiar to India, it includes 'this world' (*iham*) and 'the other worlds' (*param*) along with their inhabitants. Intuitively perceiving the above-mentioned three factors as pertaining to an integral whole should also necessarily form the essential content of any final vision of reality we arrive at. How all this is accomplished in the philosophy of Narayana Guru is what we are concerned with in the present study.

'Cosmos' means that which is well ordered though this 'orderedness' is never completely comprehensible to the human mind, for the reason that humans and their comprehending mind are simply part of the well-structured cosmos. Given that Reality is thus well-structured, any real awareness of it also has to be similarly well-structured. Likewise, Reality is a living one, it never remains an inert entity. Any real understanding of the Reality also therefore must be a living one, a living experience. How far the wisdom taught by Narayana Guru is really a living experience that fully embodies the structural perfection of Reality will also fall within the purview of the present study.

A *darśana*-context, in the normal course, involves three factors: a visioning subject called *dr̥k*, a visioned reality called *dr̥śya*, and the act of visioning called *darśana*. These three together in Vedānta are known as *tripuṭi*. The *dṛśya* in the present case is the all-underlying Reality; the *dṛk*, the one who perceives it, is nothing but a minute part of the 'all'. In other words, the subject is no more than a tiny speck of the object. The vision, therefore, in the case of *Advaita Darśana*, is of a different order. The object itself being the subject, it is a vision in which there is no relevance for *tripuṭi*. It is simply an experience of the subject merging gently in the Reality envisioned, even as a drop of water merges with the ocean. How far into the fabric of this final goal is woven proper philosophising by the Guru, is yet another aspect we will have to notice carefully in the present study.

2

The *What* of Vedānta

What are we, the students of philosophy, in search of? We are in search of knowing the Reality that underlies the world. As the knower forms an integral part of that world, the Reality that underlies the world has necessarily to be the one that underlies the knower as well.

The World

The world is understood in modern science as material. The Reality underlying it is taken for granted or rather believed to be matter. It, in some mysterious way, is a configuration of energy, a phenomenon or entity determinable neither as matter nor as non-matter nor as both. On the other hand, the existence of the world conceived in philosophy, particularly in Advaita Vedānta as Narayana Guru revisualised it, is a bipolar one — the objective phenomena perceptible to the senses forming the one pole, and the corresponding ideas or percepts formulated in the mind of the perceiver forming the other. To think of the one pole as more real or important than the other is both impossible and meaningless.

The experience of every object, we know, has involved in it the formulation of a corresponding idea in the mind. No assertion of the existence of something is possible in the absence of such a perception or ideation. Nor does the existence of such a thing have any meaning. Everything conceived of by the human mind is given a name. In a way, we thus become capable of stating that the world (*prapañca*) is constituted of innumerable concepts, innumerable names and the corresponding innumerable objects. Narayana Guru in this sense defines the world thus:

> Names in their thousands,
> concepts in their thousands,
> and the externally existing
> objects in their thousands
> corresponding to each of them —
> these together form the world.[1]

Names and concepts could well be fused together; then the world can be thought of as having the subjective realm of concepts and the objective realm of the perceived as two sides of the same coin. The Reality we are in search of is the one that underlies both the subjective and objective phenomena. To be more precise in Vedāntic terms, it is the core-Reality that unfolds itself as the subjective experience as well as the objective experience. For this reason, the ultimate Reality is neither subjective nor objective. In other words, it is not solely what is asserted by either idealism or materialism.

Every experience, we know, involves the three basic factors called *tripuṭi*. The Reality, seen from that point of view, is the one that manifests itself as the knower, the known and the act of knowing at the same time.

Every act of knowing takes place in, and is inseparable from the knower. The knower, in his turn, is an integral part of the known world. Knowing really what Reality is, therefore, in essence, is the event of the knower finding himself merged with the known, through the act of knowing, with no distinction remaining finally among the three.

What is *Ātman*? What is *Brahman*?

This Reality, in Vedānta, is known as *ātmā* or *ātman*. A word derived from the verb root *āt*, meaning to pervade the being of something (*ād vyāpane*), it signifies the Substance that pervades the being of all that has come into being. One such being is the knower himself. Therefore,

---

1. Narayana Guru, *Advaita Dīpikā*, Verse 1.

the word *ātmā* denotes the self or oneself as well. Its best English equivalant is 'the self'. In the sense of being the Substance that always grows and assumes the form of the ever-changing world, it is called *Brahman* also, a word derived from the root *bṛh* meaning, 'to grow'. *Brahman* thus literally means 'that which always grows or the all-encompassing one'. 'The Absolute' is the nearest equivalant in English. The common usage of the word *ātmā* refers to the Substance in every individuated being, and that of *Brahman* to the universal being. Realising the essential oneness of *Brahman* and *ātman* is the final goal Vedānta aims at, often referred to as *brahmātmaikyā*.

The One Substance

What in essence is this Substance referred to both as *ātman* and *Brahman*? Let us, as Narayana Guru himself does in Verse 3 of his *Advaita Dīpikā* (Lamp of Non-Duality), analyse something that forms part of the world, e.g., a piece of cloth. The cloth when analysed disappears in the being of yarn. The yarn, taken apart, disappears in the being of cotton fibres. The fibre, likewise, disappears in the being of constituent basic elements — *ākāśa* (space), *vāyu* (air), *agni* (fire), *ap* (water) and *pṛthivī* (earth). These elements, in their pure and uncompounded form, have no actual existence other than as concepts. The existence of concepts is in consciousness or mind alone. In other words, consciousness is the one Substance that manifests itself as the basic elements, as fibres, as yarn, as cloth, as everything perceptible, in short as the world. This unconditioned Consciousness, as the all-underlying Substance, is called *cit* or *samvit* in Sanskrit, and the Malayālam word the Guru prefers is *aṟivu*. The Reality we are in search of, thus, is this *cit* or *aṟivu*.

Saccidānanda

This *ātmā* at times is defined in the Upaniṣads as *saccidānanda*. Admitting the same, the Guru says in his *Darśana-Mālā* (Garland of Visions of the Absolute):

> *sarvam hi saccidānandam*
> *neha nānāsti kimca na*[2]

2. Narayana Guru, *Darśana-Mālā*, Verse 11.10.

> Everything indeed is *saccidānanda*. Multiplicity has no existence at all here.

This word is a compound of three words *sat*, *cit* and *ānanda*. *Sat* means 'existence' or that which has existence unaffected by spatial and temporal limitations. This existence is most directly experienced as one's own beingness. *Cit* means 'consciousness' or *aṟivu*, and is most intimately experienced as the self's consciousness or one's self-consciousness. How what exists ultimately is *cit* or *aṟivu* alone in essence we have just seen.

What do we ultimately gain by knowing Reality? The contentment of having found the meaning content of life, and thus the contentment of living meaningfully as freedom embodied. This ultimate contentment is what is referred to as *ānanda*. It is an experience that buds in the being of *cit*, that fills the being of *cit*. To make it short, *sat* is *cit* in essence; *ānanda* too is *cit* in essence. *Sat*, *cit* and *ānanda* are thus interchangeable terms.

Ātmā as *sat* is the Substance that manifests itself as all that appears to be, either real or unreal; as *cit*, it is the Consciousness that unfolds itself functionally as all forms of knowledge, right or wrong, as all emotions laudable or not, as all states of mind oscillating between waking and sleeping (*jāgarita* and *suṣupti*). As *ānanda* it is the measuring rod that evaluates every experience of ours as happy, painful or arousing indifference.

The *ātmā* or *Brahman* we are seeking, thus, in essence is *saccidānanda*.

3

The *How* of Vedānta (Methodology)

The seekers are ourselves. We were born as integral parts of the world; we live as integral parts of the world; we will be dying as integral parts of the functional system of the world. The Substance that underlies the being of ourselves is the same that underlies the whole. The best and the most direct way of knowing the Reality of the world, therefore, is to look for the Substance that underlies our own being. It is like in the case of a gold ornament. The best way for a gold ornament to know directly what gold is, would be for it to look into itself and see what it is made of. Then it would realise, 'I am gold', or rather 'That gold is myself'. This is the reason why all the seers always assert, the best way to know *Brahman* is by knowing *ātmā* or knowing oneself.

Interiorised Perceiving

Helping to perceive objects existing externally is what sense organs do. One seeing oneself — not one seeing one's own body — needs no sense organ; one has only to close one's eyes and other sense organs and direct one's attention towards oneself. The Substance that underlies the being even of the sense organs and their functions being what we are in search of, it can never be something the very same sense organs can get into contact with. It is for these reasons that Narayana Guru, fully in line with the Upaniṣadic *ṛṣis*, underscores that the Core-Reality is to be methodically attained by interiorising the perceptive function of the senses. The enquiry, in other words, has to be subjective.

The way of enquiry being subjecive does in no way mean that the Reality thus attained is also subjective in nature. On the contrary, it is realised to be all-pervading and all-inclusive. Subjectivity, in this context, is thus merely of methodological as opposed to ontological relevance.

Dialectics of Interiorised Perception

How is this interiorised perceiving to be effected? The Reality sought is one that appears as all phenomena both subjective and objective, the former pertaining to mind and the latter to matter. Of the Reality, these two aspects alone are recognisable. Hence these alone are the references available to lead the seeker to the Reality. Reality as such, remains imperceptible and, therefore, unreferable. The only way therefore to attain the core of the Reality is pointing out the two referable aspects to the seeker and leaving to him or her the job of intuitively perceiving what lies hidden in between. This must be accomplished on one's own. The way could well be compared to knowing what the content and value of a coin is, by making use of both its sides. Neither of the sides reveals the total content and value of the coin. Yet without both the sides the coin would be no coin, nor could it be recognised as a coin. The real value and content of it is bracketed by the two sides. *Brahman*, likewise, is a coin which has the subjective and objective aspects of appearance for its two sides or references. This subjective-objective duality is apparent both in the being of oneself and of the world as a whole. Realising that which is in between the two, that remains always as if bracketed by the two, is our goal. The two apparent aspects, in the present enquiry, are to be treated as two counterparts of a dialectical situation, somewhat like the two poles of a single magnet. Pointing out these two counterparts correctly and leaving the job of seeking and meditatively perceiving what is between those poles, which is to be done by the seeker on his or her own, is the only way open to a guide or master. This method has always been relied upon by all seers and *gurus*, even from the time of the Upaniṣads. Narayana Guru is no exception.

Subject and object are not the only discernible dialectical pairs; microcosm (*aṇu*) and macrocosm (*akhaṇḍa*) form yet another pair, and so do many others. The Guru, pointing out the paired nature of *aṇu* and *akhaṇḍa* and showing the need of the seeker transcending their duality, says thus just before concluding his most important philosophical work, *Ātmopadeśa Śatakam* (One Hunderd Verses of Self-Instruction):

> As *aṇu* and *akhaṇḍa*, as *asti* and *nāsti* (being and nothingness), it shines forth, and also as such other pairs of opposites; and the dual experience of *asti* and *nāsti* as well vanishes later, they having no existence of their own.[1]

At the very beginning of the same work, the Guru puts emphasis on the subject-object pair and on the Core-Reality that transcends both, as follows:

> In order to attain the Core-Reality that is above the ken of ordinary knowledge, and that stands out shining simultaneously as both the inner being of the knower and what is objectively outside, one should interiorise all the five senses and searchingly learn and chant (scriptures like the present one), repeatedly prostrating oneself before (this Core-Reality).[2]

The second half of the above verse clearly shows the imperativeness of the interiorised perception we discussed at the beginning of this chapter.

Intuitively perceiving the unitive Reality by making use of its own two manifest aspects of opposite nature, is the only method helpful in seeking *Brahman*, and it is called *yoga-buddhi* in the *Bhagavad-Gītā*. The one who is fully conversant with its application and its result is called *yoga-yukta*, literally the one already united through *yoga*. The implication is that the effective using of the method results in the effacement of the seeker, who becomes merged in what

---

1. Narayana Guru *Ātmopadeśa Śatakam*, Verse 96.
2. *Ibid.*, Verse 1.

is sought. The same method in the West has been well known as 'dialectics' even from the time of Plato.

Summary of the Above

The Reality searched for is *cit* in essence; the seeking mind is *cit* in essence; the seeker knowing Reality therefore means, *cit* knowing *cit*. There being no two *cits*, this knowing, in effect, is none other than the knower becoming merged in the known, or the the knower becoming the known or the other way around. It is simply an intuitive experience of the transparency of mere beingness.

The method relied on by the Guru in the search for Reality or *ātmā,* thus, apparently is that of interiorising one's perception, and then resorting to dialectical reasoning, rather than to linear logical reasoning.

Peculiarity of the Method

An all-comprehensive science has to have an all comprehensive method of enquiry or rather methodology of its own. An absolutist science has to have an absolutist method of its own. No method that works with any of the ordinary sciences we are familiar with will cope with an absolutist science that has to be a Science of all sciences.

Relying on no 'other', interiorised perception is not relative, and hence is absolutist in nature.

The self is the most certain of all entities that one is undeniably sure, exists. Therefore, knowing oneself is the surest means of knowing what Reality is.

4

The *Why* of Vedānta (Axiology)

The problem of suffering and the quest for its avoidance has always been a fundamental need in human life. The entire philosophy of Buddhism has for its basis admitting that life is suffering itself. Why do we suffer?

Sensations and experiences are either pleasant or painful. This is but natural with the eternal flux called by Narayana Guru *prapañca-pravāha*. Should this make us unhappy? It depends upon the importance we attach to sensations in life. This importance in its turn depends upon our master-interest in life. If our interest is in keeping ourselves indulgent in pleasurable objects, then of necessity we often become disappointed. Set backs to such objectives are unavoidable, given that most of the life-events are beyond the bounds of our control. These set backs cause suffering.

Where Are We Wrong?

Double-faced is our error that causes this suffering: one, we identify ourselves with our own individuated external appearance, and two, we consider our peaceful existence as depending on other entities like ourselves. A desire to extract maximum pleasure and benefit from others thus becomes an inlaid habit with us, and it is mistaken for our goal in life.

From where do we really derive our happiness? Is it from external objects, or does it well up within ourselves, with external objects as mere instruments? The latter is the case, though we remain oblivious of it being so. In short, the interest we nurture in life is an illusory one.

What Is *Ānanda*?

What should then be the unfailing interest in life? To seek happiness (*ānanda*) in oneself as welling up within oneself, as forming the essential content of one's own being. The end of this seeking is marked by realising oneself in essence as *saccidānanda*.

The goal thus has two dialectically paired aspects:

1. The negative process of eliminating suffering which itself is negative. The process thus is that of a double negation.
2. Positively attaining happiness which is of positive value. The process thus is of double assertion. This is to be attained by finding our real identity and fixing our master-interest in the *ānanda*-content of what comprises that identity.

These two are mutually complementary. One is meaningless without the other. They are the two sides of the coin of realised *ānanda*.

Living beings, life-interest-wise, are classified in the *Chāndogya Upaniṣad* into three types.[1]

1. Those who seek eternal happiness in themselves. They live an austere life preferring to be away from the din of the world of pleasure-seeking. They are seekers.
2. Those who seek pleasure from the objects of this world and of the other. To gain the former they resort to activities (*karmas*); to ensure pleasures in the latter world they perform rituals, also called *karmas*. They conceive of their existence as going up and coming down in between these two worlds of interest. They are the ignorant, though having some value concepts of their own. Their ignorance of themselves is called *ajñāna*.

---

1. *Chāndogya Upaniṣad*, Chapter V, Section 10.

3. In the case of animals and vegetables, life is guided by no thinking or value notion. Life for them is comprised simply of being born, eating, begetting, and dying.

Philosophy, at least as understood in Vedānta, is meant for those of the first category.

The traditionally held ultimate goal of Vedāntic enquiry is attaining *mokṣa*, meaning 'Liberation' — liberation from everything that binds one. All such bondages in general are signified by the term *bandha*. Liberation thus is from all *bandha*s.

*Bandha*s eventually end up in making life fearful. Therefore, to become free of all fears (*bhaya*) is thought of as another facet of the final goal of Vedānta, and the goal on this account is known as *abhaya* (fearlessness).

Although everyone is well aware of its inevitability, the most terrific of all fears in life is that of death *(mr̥tyu)*. How to attain immortality? This, in a sense, is one thing everyone aspires for. Is it possible to attain immortality even as death has its natural role in the on-going creative process of nature? Vedānta's answer is positive. Enabling the seeker to attain immortality in the absolute sense, is yet another aspect of the purpose of Vedānta. The goal in this respect is known as *amr̥tatva* (immortality).

To go back again to the problem of suffering, why is it that some are destined to lead a miserable life for no fault of their own? Why is it that some others apparently live happy and comfortable lives in spite of being involved in not-so-good activities? Is it because of their *karma*s of previous births, as is popularly held? What then is *karma*? What is its role in deciding the future of the individual as well as of the world? How can one become free of such *karma*s? To make one free from all such entangling *karma*s and the resultant reincarnations, is yet another facet of Vedānta's goal.

All these, though differently stated, are not different goals. They simply are one goal differently viewed. Attaining that one goal is what we are after in the present study.

5

We Prepare Ourselves

The wisdom under consideration here is not meant for all, nor is it desired by all. The thirsty alone enjoy drink. The hungry alone relish food. Zest for knowing the meaning of life alone makes wisdom worth pursuing.

With a few, the quest for wisdom arises as a natural, in-born trait. With many, it arises as the aftermath of some unexpected, untoward event that transforms the course of life altogether. Such situations compel them to think, 'What is the meaning of life?', 'Why should I live?', 'Why was I even born?', 'Is there anything that makes my existence meaningful?', 'If so, what is it, where is it?' 'Living seems meaningless unless I get a clear answer to all these questions.'

Such a one thus turns out to be a seeker. Finally, the meaning of life is found within oneself, as the Reality that unfolds itself as all events and that witnesses all events. Engrossed in a restless race for a restful existence as they are, lost in the ecstacy of capturing and enjoying whatever enjoyable objects befall them, people ordinarily remain oblivious of the one all-unfolding *sat* within themselves, the one all-witnessing *cit* they are in essence, and the one *ānanda* that manifests as all pains and pleasures.

The Prerequisites

The search for a deeper meaning in life is often precipitated by the realisation that whatever causes pain and pleasure in life and whatever seems to guide one's life, is of momentary existence only, and that the pains and pleasures thus aroused are also transitory. What one seeks is something eternal that assures eternal happiness.

Discriminating the eternal from the transient becomes thus natural with such a one. This trait is known as *nitya-anitya-viveka*.

When this discrimination becomes stabilised, spontaneously one feels an aversion or sense of detachment towards everything fleeting. This is always complemented and compensated by the aspiration for that which is eternal. This disposition preliminary to attaining wisdom is known as *vairāgya* or *nirveda*.

Once the above-said attitudes become well rooted naturally in the seeker, they are further to be strengthened by certain nurtured disciplines. These are *śama* (restraining mind from temptations), *dama* (restraining sense organs from tempting objects of pleasure), *uparati* (non-dependence on anything external in day-to-day activities), *titikṣā* (willingness to endure all sufferings and hardships with no complaining), *śraddhā* (full faith in the truthfulness of what the *guru* and scriptures teach), and *samādhāna* (to keep always the ultimate goal of attaining *Brahman* as the master guiding principle in life's progression). These six self-imposed disciplines together are known as *śamādi-ṣaṭka-sampatti*.

Finally, one should feel the indefatigable zeal to be freed from all *bandhas*. This desire for freedom is known as *mumukṣutva*, and one who is endowed with this aspiration is called *mumukṣu*.

All these prerequisites together, known as *sādhanā-catuṣṭaya-sampatti* (the four-staged self-discipline), are recommended by Narayana Guru in the first verse of his Sanskrit work, *Brahmavidyā Pañcakam* (*Brahmavidyā* in Five Verses).

Is it possible for all seekers endowed with all these prerequisites to attain *jñāna* or wisdom? With some, 'yes', and with some others, 'no'. The former type, as best exemplified by the Guru himself, guided by some inner calling and inborn gifts, subject themselves to austere self-purification that finally lands up in the dawning of the transparency of wisdom. The latter type need the guidance of an already enlightened person called *guru*.

Teaching wisdom is not the same as ordinary teaching. It is simply an assistance rendered by one who is already enlightened as to the self, to a seeker of the self. What the *guru* knows is what *ātmā* or his own self really is. What the seeker is after is knowing the Reality that he really is. A *guru* can reveal through teaching what he or she knows only, that is, his or her own self-knowledge. The disciple's objective is knowing himself, not knowing who the *guru* really is. Enlightenment in the disciple has therefore to dawn through a process in which the *guru*'s self-knowledge gets transformed as the disciples's self-knowledge. This does not take place unless a complete rapport or bipolarity, known as *guru-śiṣya-pārasparya* is established between the two. It includes the willingness on the part of the disciple (*śiṣya*) even to be always at the *guru*'s service.

All the above-said prerequisites are put together suggestively in a summary fashion in Verses 7 and 8 of Narayana Guru's *Ātmopadeśa Śatakam*. The seeker should, he says, be endowed with an inner clarity that impels him to shoot down the five birds (sense organs) that perch evasively on the tree of the barrel-like body, intent on relishing its five fruits. Unrelenting and uncompromising should be the willingness to do so. Between the lines of these two verses we read that the seeker has to make use of his own bodily existence to transcend the limitations of the very same bodily existence.

Tapas

The process of an ardent seeker's intense self-enquiry is often referred to as *tapas* in the Upaniṣads. The word literally means 'heating up'. A well disciplined self-enquiry is a self-heating-up process. In practice, it is thought of as involving living in secluded places, often caves, in order to make the constant self-heating-up distractionless. Implicit in it is an agony of some sort, pushed on by an intensity of search, full of alertness, supported by clear memory, willingness to give full attention to the problem at hand, the power to listen and the will to believe with correct scepticism, well-balanced by belief for its basis.

The picture of this *tapas* yet remains incomplete unless the seeker's self-heating-up in search of the Reality in oneself, is seen as forming only the reverse of a coin. Its obverse is the *tapas Brahman* undergoes aimed at emanating the well-ordered world from within itself. The seeker is simply one of the countless beings thus emanated. The seeker now undergoes the same *tapas* in order to realise back the *Brahman*-Reality that assumed the seeker's own form.

Yet another picture of *tapas* familiar to the Indian mind is that of a *yogī* sitting meditating under a tree — a picture that reminds us of the pre-historic Śaiva tradition. The same picture with a revised and revalued dimension is portrayed by the Guru in Verse 9 of *Ātmopadeśa Śatakam*. The tree in it is none other than *māyā*-tree and it is overgrown by a bushy creeper in bloom, that has two branches which are the subjective and objective aspects of appearance we have already seen. One who successfully undergoes such a *tapas* alone transcends the world of sins (*pāpa*s) and the resultant inevitability of having to live in hell (*naraka*). Put otherwise, winning over *māyā* is to be accomplished by making use of the very same *māyā* as a tool or protective shade. How this works is a point to be clarified later.

Sin and Merit

What are sin and merit (*pāpa* and *puṇya*) in the Vedāntic perspective? Not seeing oneself as an inalienable part of the whole, not seeing oneself as a transitory manifest form of the one all-underlying Reality, and thus living a life guided by interests in fleeting pleasures, unmindful of others, unmindful of the whole, is *pāpa* (sin). One who does so, by doing so, is transforming his own life in this world into a *naraka* (hell).

A discriminating mind, on the other hand, aspires for the eternal Reality in one's own transient form, transforms one's own life as a means, a *tapas*, for attaining the eternal, and thus realises incessant *ānanda*, the vicissitudes of actual events in life notwithstanding. Such is the one who makes a heaven of one's own life. This is the way of *puṇya* (merit).

6

The Search

The method for seeking Reality has to be subjectively oriented for the reason that the Substance that forms one's own being is that Reality. All inclusive, that Substance has to be perceived dialectically as well. That is to say, any conceivable existential context is to be perceived as bracketed by two extreme poles of opposite nature. Moreover, such a methodology, in application, should be becoming to the spirit of the Age of Science of which Narayana Guru was a product.

The well-acknowledged and most respected method of scientific enquiry is experimentation. But would it be possible to subject *ātmā* to any sort of experimentation? The Guru says, 'Yes'. How is it? Let us see. Our purpose is to know oneself. The 'I' in myself is *ātmā*. Literally too, the word *aham*, meaning 'I', and *ātmā* are synonyms.

What do scientists actually do in an experiment to arrive at a definite conclusion? First, they set up a laboratory with all the equipment needed for the particular experiment, along with the thing to be experimented upon. Then they perform the actual experiment. Secondly, they collect all the required data from what is observed. And finally, they make calculations based on those data. With the spirit of the Age of Science having been imbibed, as was seen earlier in the case of analysing a piece of cloth with a view to finding out what ultimately underlies the being of everything, the Guru once again sets up an experimental situation like that of a controlled laboratory.

The Experiment

The laboratary is a dark room. Nothing distinct is visible there. Two persons are sitting in it, each not knowing of the presence of the other. One, suspecting the presence of someone else also in the room, asks, 'Who are you sitting in darkness?' 'I', the reply comes, and he in return asks, 'Who are you?' Again the reply comes, 'I'. This much is the actual experiment.

Now the datum required is easily collected: that the question, 'Who are you?' is answered by both as 'I'. That means, a common 'I' is there in both. Not only in these two, but in all individual beings there should be this one common 'I'. The most modern findings of science confirm that there is nothing in this world that has no element of consciousness in it. What is that one commom 'I'? That 'I' or *aham* should be the *ātmā.*

Calculations

From this point we begin the real calculation, the third step:

Multiplicity of beings is what we apparently see. Are we really many? Is the 'I' in each of us one or many? The observation from the experiment is that one 'I' is there in many. This one 'I' is seen only when each of us looks at ourselves ignoring all the visible factors as in a dark room. The divergence of this one 'I' into many 'I's happens only when looked at externally. Of these two types of perceiving, the latter is conditioned by such factors as mind, sense organs, physical body and so on, and therefore the knowledge of the 'I' attained is also conditioned. Such conditioning factors are known as *upādhi*s, and the knowledge thus conditioned, *sopādhika-jñāna*. All such *upādhi*s are of a fleeting nature; the knowledge conditioned by them, i.e., *sopādhika-jñāna,* is also transient. All the multitude of 'I's therefore exists only for a short while.

The one 'I'-consciousness in all, on the other hand, is subject to no conditioning. This self-knowledge with no conditioning is called *nirupādhika-jñāna*. It is simple, pure awareness felt within, although the withinness itself has also vanished. It is like one perceiving oneself as the centre of a circle of effulgence with infinity for its circumference, and the centre vanished. This common 'I' never ceases to be, because life never ceases to be. Having no conceivable bounds, it is complete in itself (*pūrṇa*).

It is in and through the emerging and merger of the countless fleeting 'I's that the boundless being of the eternal 'I' finds existential expression.

The aggregate of all such expressions, having a structural perfection of its own, in its state of active existence, is called *prakṛti*, loosely translatable as 'nature' in English. The word *prakṛti* as defined by the Guru himself in his *Darśana-Mālā* (IV. 10) means, "that which is in a self-activated state" (*prakarṣeṇa karoti iti prakṛtiḥ*).

What is the result of this self-activation? The three *guṇas* — *sattva*, *rajas* and *tamas* — become apparent. Our ordinary existence as individuals is as part of this *prakṛti* and is thus subject to the three *guṇas* as is the existence of its counterpart — the cosmic system. Therefore, the *ātmā* we are seeking, the Reality that underlies both, has necessarily to be something that transcends the three *guṇas*. This transcending is symbolically conceived as reducing them to ashes. The Śaiva custom of wearing ashes on the forehead and sometimes on various other parts of the body, signifies this.

The *prakṛti*, in its 'nature natured' (actualised) form, as against its 'nature naturing' (potential) form, is what we call 'the world'. How many such worlds are there? The Vedas conceive of three worlds: *bhūḥ*, *bhuvaḥ* and *suvaḥ* (the Earth, the Middle World, the Heaven), also called *bhūmi*, *antarikṣa* and *svarga*. The mythological legends of India sometimes count the number of worlds as fourteen and very rarely as twenty one. Modern science, on the other hand, thinks, such worlds in the ever expanding universe are innumerable. The Reality we seek, the 'I' in me, the 'I' in the being of all the worlds, ontologically has to be one that underlies all these worlds, and at the same time is beyond all the worlds.

We are now engrossed in the act of seeking. Involved in all seeking are a seeker, that which is sought, and the act of seeking, together known as *ṭripuṭi*. Seen epistemologically, therefore, the Reality has to be the one that underlies and is beyond *ṭripuṭi*. It is thus not something that could be known as an object.

The Finding

What kind of knowledge then is that of *ātmā*? Neither realistic nor idealistic, *ātmā*, when known, is not objective nor is it subjective (the best method of search for it being subjective notwithstanding). It simply can be an ineffable experience of inner clarity in which the seeker, the sought and the seeking merge in the beingness of one all-engulfing effulgence; it is an experience of an inner eye getting opened; it is the fruition of one's meditative pondering on what hides unsaid in a *guru*'s instructions. This opening up is experienced as you finding yourself floating in a flood that overflows everywhere, where before there existed only an expansive wasteland.

What is the *ātmā* known thuswise? How is it defined? The Guru gives a clear definition in positive terms as to what it is, as opposed to what it is not, as is done traditionally in Advaita Vedānta.

> That which, while remaining in darkness, is conscious of itself, is called *ātmā*; it is none other than pure and unconditioned Consciousness (*aṟivu*) in essence. It is this *aṟivu*, magically indeed, that unfolds itself as all the names, all the forms, all the mental faculties, all sense organs, all activities, all doers of action, in short, as all the worlds.[1]

The 'darkness' in which *aṟivu* remains or is seated, referred to in this definition, reminds us of the darkness the two persons of the above experiment were sitting in.

The world does not exist apart from that *aṟivu*, even as ornaments do not exist apart from gold. The insistence made by many as to the self as 'this' or 'that', whatever the logically tenable reason supporting their claims, marks simply lack of clear vision on their part. The world's existence and its incessant creativity, is not logic-based; on the other hand, logic and reasoning merely derive from it.

1. Narayana Guru, *Ātmopadeśa Śatakam*, *op. cit.*, Verse 27.

Logical thinking may take us to different conclusions depending on the premises we start from, the course of thinking we pursue, and finally our interest or value notion. The one who has attained the proper and integral vision of *ātmā,* on the other hand, argues for or against no particular theory or 'ism' concerning the Real; instead, he remains fully merged in what he has found. Many are the possibilities of reasoning going wrong, and thus of formulating many theories or 'isms', but the right vision can be only one. Formulating such theories about something does in no way affect the being of that 'something'.

In short, the certain and clear vision of *ātmā* is not the outcome of any logically tenable means of knowledge (*pramāṇa*s), but is an experiential illumined-ness. This is where the Guru's scientific-like experiment has ultimately landed us.

Narayana Guru's philosophical vision thus is a ground where both science and mysticism meet each other and merge together, one supporting the other, one validating the other.

7

The Individual

An individual living being is designated in Sanskrit by the word *jīva*. Derived from the root *jīv* meaning 'to survive through breathing' (*jīva-prāṇadhāraṇe*), it is the Sanskrit equivalent to the modern word 'organism'. So I can say, 'I am a *jīva*'; not, 'I have a *jīva*'. Perhaps for the reason that the word is mixed up in common usage with the theological concept 'soul', the Guru in his philosophical works avoids it.

The role of an individual in life, particularly a human individual, is as a *jñātā* (knower), a *kartā* (doer of actions), and a *bhoktā* (enjoyer). We will have to deal with these aspects in detail, later.

The Origin

How does the individual originate? Our scientific knowledge and common sense do not take us beyond the fact that an individual's birth is from the sexual union of parents. This birth-phenomenon is merely a minute part of an overall structurally perfect scheme of life ordained by no-one-knows-who. Religionists call that source-mind 'God'. The Guru, while not disagreeing with religionists, thinks of it, as the Upaniṣadic *ṛṣi*s also did, as *ātmā* of which nothing can be predicated. *Ātmā,* in other words, is the original source, the material cause as well as the efficient cause, of the world and of the individual as well.

Ātmā always remains unknown. The coming into being of an individual from that unknown Reality, is portrayed in the *Chāndogya Upaniṣad* as a five-tiered *yajña* (fire sacrifice) beginning with the *yajña* that takes place in the unknown above and ending with the union of parents here, which is also presented as a *yajña*. For all these five *yajña*s there is a common set of priests: the *deva*s, gods of heaven. They symbolise knowledge in its functional state. The same picture, in a poetico-scientific manner, is drawn by the Guru by comparing the emerged individual human being to a two-tiered oil lamp. Hanging on a chain hooked to the unknown above, it has five petals in each tier, each petal with a burning wick and provided with sufficient supply of oil.

The unknown beginning is indistinct as well; so is the end of the individual too. It being so is suggested by the long chain hooked to the beginningless. The same chain is to be seen as extending downwards also to the endless. In between the indistinct and beginningless top and the indistinct and endless bottom exists the tiny, seemingly distinct, evanescent, always active individual, represented by the ever-rotating lamp (shown at page no. 30). The subjective and objective aspects of our existence and knowledge, or the mental and physical facets of our being, are symbolically signified by the two tiers. Each is meaningless without the other.

The two tiers have five petals each: the five sense organs on the subject side and the corresponding objects on the other. The mental faculties and organs of action are also added. All this together functioning as an organic unit, forms the individual: the *jñātā*, the *kartā*, and the *bhoktā*.

A wick burns at each of the petals; it is none other than the function (*vṛtti*) of each of the senses, mental faculties, or organs of action. These flames derive their energy from the oil of *vāsanā*s, the impressions left behind by previous experiences in the store-house of mind. How such *vāsanā*s are handed down through a long line of generations, controlling the character and life pattern of each individual, is a factor well acknowledged even by modern genetics. How old such *vāsanā*s are, we don't know. One thing is sure: they are linked to the very beginningless.

And now, what constitutes the total figure, both the physical and mental aspects included, of the lamp? It is just a shade. No shade, no matter how visibly apparent, has an existence of its own.

Shade is just an obstruction caused to the free flow of light-rays. Likewise, the free flow of the effulgence of *aṟivu* faces a self-caused obstruction, that of *avidyā,* which we'll be dealing within a moment. An individual's existence, in other words, is a shade-like one, with all the above-mentioned activities and functions taking place in it. Such a mystery is what we call 'the individual'. Lo and behold, it is the other pole of the other mystery called 'the world'!

The Simplest Fact

In spite of the fact that it has the shade-creating *avidyā* always present within it, *ātmā* is in essence pure effulgence. As part of that effulgence manifesting itself, 'I' the individual too is, in essence, effulgence. The simplest of all directly experienced facts therefore is that 'I' or *aham* is not darkness at all; it is effulgence in content. An open secret, this is to be declared to all!

'I' and the world are nothing more than two apparent, opposite facets — particular and universal — of the manifest form of one *ātmā*, effulgence in essence. The two, in other words, are dialectical counterparts of the one functional existence of *ātmā*. With this perception attained, I begin to see myself in everything in the world, and everything in myself. Then I realise that the world has no existence apart from me. Whatever appears as existing in the form of the world is nothing but myself, nothing but *ātmā*. Mistaking a beautiful flower garland for a snake does not make it a snake; it remains garland even when seen as a snake. Likewise, even when seen as the world, what exists really, *ātmā,* continues to exist as *ātmā*.

Ātmā's self-manifesting, though appearing as having two dialectically opposite facets, has a structural coherence and perfection of its own. At both extremes of this well-arranged system, numerous details are discernible, either microcosmic or macrocosmic. Who keeps this system structurally perfect and alive? The *ātmā* itself. Already imprinted in *ātmā*, so to say, are all such structural details. *Ātmā,* in other words, is the creator, sustainer and destroyer of the worlds. It could well be conceived in this context that *ātmā* and God mean the same. The Malayālam word for God, *daivam,* also means 'that which is effulgence in essence'. It derives from the root *div* meaning 'to be luminous'. The Sanskrit word for God, *īśvara,* means 'the all-controller', for it derives from the root *īś,* meaning 'to be in control'.

Vidyā and *Avidyā*

Though I am really this *ātmā,* I remain oblivious of being so. Instead of seeing myself as *ātmā*, I think I am so and so. Because of this mistaken identity, all sense of separateness arises. This separateness, in its turn, results in love and hatred, all sorts of bondages (*bandha*), and all fears (*bhaya*). There is an element of negativity that hides itself in our consciousness. It is known as *avidyā*. It is defined as that functional element of consciousness, caused by *māyā*, because of which you do not see yourself as *ātmā*, but you see yourself identified with the external form in which you appear to be, often referred to as *anātmā* (non-self). To make it clear, that which impels a piece of ornament to see itself as that ornament, not as gold, is *avidyā*. The wrong kind of knowledge caused by this *avidyā* is called *ajñāna*.

Now, what is *vidyā*? Just as an ornament knowing itself as gold, you may see yourself as *ātmā*, instead of seeing as so and so different from all else. That element in consciousness that impels you to see thus is *vidyā*. *Vidyā*, in its turn, helps you attain *jñāna*. We have already seen what sort of experience *jñāna* is.

Turīya

The final stage of this *jñāna* attained is known as *turīya*. What is *turīya*? A description of it is given in the *Māṇḍūkya Upaniṣad* in terms of what it is not, rather than as what it is. Narayana Guru, on the other hand, gives a clear yet mystical definition of it in terms of what it is, in Verse 28 of *Ātmopadeśa Śatakam*. According to him, it is an experience of one becoming enlightened of the being of oneself from tip to bottom; it is also an experience of one becoming enlightened of the being of the world from beginning to end, or rather from the beginningless to the endless. Otherwise put, it is the experience of clearly visioning from beginning to end, that which is beginningless and endless.

At this fruition of *vidyā*, one ceases to be a *jñātā*, *kartā* and *bhoktā*. One's notion, 'I am a *jñātā*', 'I am a *kartā*', 'I am a *bhoktā*', in other words, is an outcome of *avidyā*.

8

KARMA

As we have seen, the function of individual human beings is as *jñātā*, *kartā*, and *bhoktā*. Let us now concentrate on the *kartā* aspect.

Kartā is the performer of *karmas*; and *karma* goes on everywhere in *prakṛti*. In fact *prakṛti* is not *prakṛti* without *kṛti* (action), another word for *karma*.

Karma is apparent in the realms of both the universal and the particular. Water flows, fire blazes, wind blows, rain pours down, the earth supports everything — all these are universal *karmas*. Luminaries in their thousands move around in the outer space, supernovae explode, stars emerge and remerge — these are *karmas* of cosmic dimension.

You breathe, you eat, you drink, the food eaten gets digested, blood circulates, sense organs function, mind thinks, wills, imagines and becomes emotional — all these are *karmas* related to the individual. Sub-atomic particles function in different, already fixed ways to form a perfectly functioning system called an atom; this *karma* is of the microcosmic level.

Together, all these form the functional existence of *prakṛti*. The well-known 'eternal flux' thus is an eternal flow of *karmas*.

What is *Karma?*

Prakṛti is in an incessantly changing state. Every change involves an event taking place. Every event is an outcome of an action (*karma*) that takes place in that context. *Karma*, individually seen, is the inner urge in an entity to transform itself from one state of existence into another. This urge is there in everything; therefore events take place everywhere. Universally seen, *karma* is the inner urge in the ultimate Reality, *ātmā*, to cause specific entities to emerge from itself, as is well-defined as follows in the *Bhagavad Gītā*:

> *bhūta-bhāvodbhava-karo* ।
> *visargaḥ karma-saṁjñitaḥ.* ॥[1]

> This is to be understood by the word *karma*: the specific creative urge that causes the coming into being of all that has come into being.

Where is the abode of this *karma*? In the imperishable *ātmā*. Narayana Guru, therefore says:

> *ātmaiva māyayā karma* ।
> *karoti bahu-rūpa-dhṛk.* ॥[2]

> *Ātmā* indeed, assuming various forms, does all *karma*s because of *māyā*.

This *karma*-urge in *ātmā*, when activated, is called *prakṛti*. *Ātmā* and *prakṛti*, therefore, are not two realities. The one Reality thought of as existing virtually, is *ātmā*. The same actually existing, self-actualised, is called *prakṛti*.

Individual's *Karma*

Our individual existence is as part of the total existence of *prakṛti*. *Prakṛti* is active. Forming part of it, we are also active. The total action of *prakṛti* as well as all individual actions simply form part of the one eternal flow of *karma*s. Individuals as such, therefore, have no *karma* of their own. The *Bhagavad Gītā* categorically tells us:

> *prakṛteḥ kriyamāṇāni guṇaiḥ karmāṇi sarvaśaḥ* ।
> *ahaṁkāra-vimūdhātmā kartāham iti manyate* ॥[3]

---

1. *Bhagavad Gītā*: VIII. 3.
2. Narayana Guru, *op. cit., Darśana-Mālā*: VI. 1.
3. *Bhagavad Gītā*: III. 27, *loc. cit.*

> *Karmas* take place everywhere because of the *guṇas* of *prakṛti*. The deluded one, because of egoity, thinks, 'I am the doer of *karmas*'.

Who then is the doer of *karmas*? Virtually, *ātmā* is the doer. Actually, *prakṛti* is the doer.

No individual, even those who are thought of as doers of meritorious deeds, can escape the necessity of the overall *karma*. Narayana Guru therefore says:

> Even those of meritorious action (*sukṛtis*) are helplessly caught in the whirling action of *prakṛti* and thus do revolve.[4]

Given that the individual has no *karma*, the problem of *pāpa* and *puṇya* also vanishes. *Prakṛti*'s *karmas* on their own are neither good *karma* nor bad *karmas*, they are just *karmas*.

How *Karma* Works

The *karma*-urge in *ātmā* results in the emerging of the world from itself. The same *karma* works in the dissolution of every entity thus emerged as well. The dissolution of one form becomes the emergence of another, just as the death of the egg becomes the birth of the chick. Life goes on thus unhindered, enriched by birth and death. Narayana Guru gives a complete picture of it in his *Ātmopadeśa Śatakam*:

> As with waves in ocean, individuated entities, one after another, do emerge and merge back. Lo and behold, this does not end! It is just the ceaseless *karma* that inheres in the primeval ocean of *samvit* (consciousness).[5]

Life seen wholly is thus the process by which one Reality, *ātmā*, *saccidānanda* in essence, endures endlessly through the ever-repeating births and deaths of individuated forms that emerge from itself.

---

4. Narayana Guru, *op. cit.*, *Ātmopadeśa Śatakam*: Verse 43.
5. *Op. cit.*, Verse 56.

Free Will

No individual, then, really is the doer of any *karma*. Even free will and its application are in humans as part of *prakṛti*. The free and wilful decisions we take are also *prakṛti* functioning. It is as ordained by *prakṛti* that we are endowed with these qualities. The best of all usages of free will, therefore, will be in making our own life's existence and flow to be one with that of the cosmic system, something on which we have no control at all and of which we know very little.

Avidyā and *Karma*

That I am a doer of actions is an illusory notion. It is caused by *avidyā*. This is the reason why *avidyā* and *karma* are always linked together in Vedānta. Rituals also, we know, are called *karma*s. They are performed by those who consider themselves as their doers. They expect some favourable personal gain also as a result. They too are guided by *avidyā*.

If I realise myself as being *ātmā*, then I personally have no *karma* of my own. *Ātmā* alone has *karma*s. *Ātmā*, the all underlying Substance, has no sense of agency of action (*kartṛtva*). Its *karma*s, therefore, are virtually no *karma*, or it in effect becomes *akarma* (non-action). A self-realised person's *karma*s, in other words, turn out to be *akarma*s or non-actions. This is what is true in the case of those who follow the path of *vidyā*.

If I consider myself as so and so, an individually-existing person, then I have *karma*. I then become bound to eat its fruits (*karma-phala*), whether sweet or bitter. This is meaningful only for those who are not yet free from *avidyā*. The *Bhagavad Gītā* also underscores this point when it says:

> *na kartṛtvam na karmāṇi lokasya sṛjati prabhuḥ* ।
> *na karma-phala-saṁyogam svabhāvas tu pravartate* ॥[6]

No sense of agency of action (*kartṛtva*), no *karma* either, has been ordained for any individual being of the world, by the

---

6. *Bhagavad Gītā*: V. 14, *op. cit.*

> Overlord. Nor is ordained any predetermined union with fruits of action. What works is only the inherent nature of what really exists.

To sum up, *karmas* by themselves, are unreal (*asat*). Reality (*sat*) is that which underlies all *karmas*, all individuals and the entire world. That is what *jñānins* find themselves fully identified with.

Classification of *Karmas*

Given that *karmas* are unreal, how can they be classified? Something real alone can be classified. Categorising something unreal does not make any sense. Of course, with those who are unwilling to be freed from *avidyā,* such classification may sound good. It is not the case with the seeker as well as with the enlightened. Addressing the former, the latter says, in the words of Narayana Guru:

> *prārabdham kva nu sañcitam tava*
> *kim āgāmi kva karmāpy asat* ।
> *tvayi adhyastam ato'khilam tvam asi*
> *saccin mātram ekam vibhuḥ* ॥[7]

> How can you have *prārabdha-karma*? How can you have *sañcita-karma*? How can you have *āgāmi-karma*? *Karma* itself is unreal. All such notions are simply superimposed on you. You simply are the one manifesting-as-all *sat-cit*.

Yet the popular notion among all schools of Vedānta is that every *jīva* has to suffer *sañcita-karmas* (residues of actions done in past lives), *āgāmi-karmas* (*karmas* still in the process of getting accumulated) and *prārabdha-karmas* (*karmas* already begun but the fruits not yet eaten). Even *jñānins*, it is held, are not free from the last one. The apparent reason upheld to justify this belief is the phenomenon sometimes seen in the lives of saints in which they are made to suffer great bodily pains, especially towards the end of their lives.

---

7. Narayana Guru, *op. cit.*, *Brahmavidyā Pañcakam*, Verse 5.

Why should we insist on explaining everything? Why can't it be counted as pertaining to *māyā*? This word, we know, is used by Vedāntins simply to admit that certain basic things are inexplicable. Why can't we remain satisfied that the variety of *prakṛti*'s *karma*s are such that some happen to face pains more than others? To be true, such pains, pleasures as well, do not make any change in the perception of *jñānin*s. Admitting actual events as unavoidable, whether painful or pleasurable, and as pertaining only to *prakṛti*, and thus facing them with a sense of equanimity — this is what is natural with *jñānin*s. *Ajñānin*s alone feel it necessary to explain the apparent sufferings people undergo, and think a *jñānin* has always to be painless.

What is our goal? Is it to finish with all the three types of *karma*s one by one and then attain liberation? Or, is it to liberate ourselves from *avidyā* that makes such *karma*s and their classification meaningful? Although the latter is the case, still many, even great *ācārya*s, seem to forget it.

Rebirth

Another problem, also understood as closely related to an individual's *karma*s, is that of rebirth. Rebirth becomes meaningful only where birth and death are also so. The latter two, we know, are seen to be real only because of *avidyā*, for the Reality in every apparent being was never born and it never dies. *Avidyā* makes one identify oneself with one's evanescent apparent form and mistake its emerging as birth and re-merger as death.

Released from *avidyā*, one finds both birth and death as unreal. When death vanishes, rebirth becomes meaningless. Therefore, rebirth is only meaningful within the realm of *avidyā*, i.e., within the realm of the unreal. Rebirth, ultimately, is unreal. Narayana Guru categorically says:

> No death, no birth, no life-span, no humans, no gods; what seem to be so are mere names and forms.[8]

---

8. Narayana Guru, *op. cit.*, *Ātmopadeśa Śatakam*, Verse 78.

These names and forms become configured in the one *aṟivu* owing to the *karma* inherent in it. Seen as that *aṟivu* or *ātmā*, I was never born and I'll never die. For the one all-underlying Substance is birthless and deathless. This vision, this enlightenment, makes me immortal (*amṛta*), one who has transcended death.

Seen as so and so, I was born and am destined to die. The problem, 'What will happen to me after death?' poses itself before me only in that context. The popular concept of rebirth attempts to solve this ignorance-caused problem in such a way as to satisfy the ignorant — not to make them enlightened. But no *darśana* is aimed at making you ignorant or keeping you ignorant; it does not try to teach you what is unreal. On the contrary, its goal is making you enlightened as to the Real. Any reference to the unreal by way of teaching you what the real is, does not form the proper teaching. Reference to birth, death, and rebirth in our scriptures are of this category. In order to keep us away from the danger of mixing up these two, Narayana Guru avoided any reference to rebirth in his philosophical thinking.

How the Guru perceives the phenomena of birth and death we have already seen with the help of the analogy of waves and ocean. One ocean, remaining unchanged, emanates waves within itself. The rising of each wave is its birth; its disappearance is its death. Likewise is the ocean of *samvit* or *aṟivu*. An individual being is a wave that arises within it. Its arising is what we call birth, and its merger, death. Really nothing is born there, nothing dies there. Yet the *karma* inherent in *aṟivu* or *ātmā* makes new wave-like individuals arise and disappear. The *ātmā* remains immortal throughout.

Each wave's magnitude, force and character depend to some extent on the magnitude, force and character of the one that arose just before. That means, the *karma* inherent in one wave is carried on to the next one. This process continues endlessly. The same is the case with what happens in the ocean of *samvit*. In this limited sense, it is not untrue that the birth of one individual depends to a great extent on the course of *karma* that preceded its coming into being. The bodily features, psychological peculiarities, and many such characteristics of children, depend to a great extent on those of their parents. Some of what the parents did in their life are also transmitted to their children through genes. Thus, the notion that the emergence of beings happens as dictated by the course of *karma*s in general is quite acceptable even to modern science.

The *Karma-Yogī*

A *jñānin* is a *yogin* (*yogī*) as well. *Yogī* means he who sees himself as one with the whole, one with *ātmā*. He sees whatever he does as the *karma* of the one all-underlying Reality becoming unfolded. The words *yoga* and *yogī* are derived from the verb root *yuj* meaning 'to unite two together'. For the *yogī*, whatever he does becomes transformed as a means to realise his oneness with the Reality. Those who thus become *yogī*s, with *karma* as a means, are known as *karma-yogī*s.

9

The World

A *karma-yogī,* too, in terms of 'the actual', is an individual. He does not exist apart from the whole; his *karma* is just part of the *karma* of the whole. All individuated entities, along with their *karma*s, taken together is called the world. Yet, it is not the sum total of the many; it is something more, having a well-structured existence and a functional system of its own, even as a body's biological existence is something more than the sum total of body cells. Let us now concentrate on that total world.

As we have already noticed, the world is the apparent concrete form assumed by the one abstract Reality, *ātmā* or *aṟivu*. This apparent form includes both physical and mental factors.

This world, being such, is in a ceaseless process of rolling on, like a wheel. This cyclic process is less like that of a machine's flywheel than it is like the wheels of a chariot. Always moving on, it advances while being cyclic in action. This is a sort of sport that *ātmā* endlessly plays. Why? We'll see in a moment.

The *What* of the World

The most fundamental categories into which the world is analysed in the Upaniṣads are *nāma* and *rūpa* (names and forms). Giving it a modern touch, Narayana Guru at one point describes the world as constituted of countless names, countless percepts and concepts, and countless corresponding perceptible objects.

What is a name? It is just an oral or written sign devised by mind or consciousness, to denote some particular percept or concept formulated in the same mind. It arises from knowledge; its function is that of easing the process of knowing through communication; its value, too, is in the context of knowing.

What is *rūpa* or form? A percept has a form, and so does a concept. The perceived or conceived object also has a form. A right knowledge of something occurs when the subjectively experienced form fully corresponds with the objective one. The subjective form and objective form are merely two dialectical counterparts of the non-dual situation of form-experience. This form-experience, on its turn, is simply a mode of appearance that arises in the one *aṟivu*. That what we call an external object also has existence only as consciousness, we have already seen with the help of the analogy of analysing a piece of cloth. Form, in other words, also has its being in *aṟivu* alone.

Thus, the world constituted of names and forms also does not have existence apart from *aṟivu*.

World as 'the Effect'

Thinking in terms of cause and effect is the most admired scientific way of searching for reality for both scientists and philosophers. Still, it should be pointed out that the logically convincing reason that makes this so has never been presented.

Causality-wise, the world is an effect. What then is its cause? Clay is the material cause (*upādāna-kāraṇa*) of pots, and the potter is their efficient cause (*nimitta-kāraṇa*). *Ātmā,* being the only Substance that has real existence, necessarily has to be the material cause of the world. As there is nothing else existing to serve as the efficient cause, *ātmā* has to be world's efficient cause as well. *Ātmā* then is the material-cum-efficient cause of the world.

A pot has no existence apart from clay. Likewise, the world has no existence of its own apart from *ātmā*. In other words, the world on its own is unreal, *asat*. How can the unreal have an origin? How can it have a dissolution? What is the originless and dissolutionless? It is *ātmā* alone. *Ātmā* alone exists and appears as the world. Birth and death, creation and dissolution, are mere illusory visions seen in *ātmā* because of *māyā*.

The *How* of the World

Even when the world is admitted as something real, its origin remains inexplicable, to scientists as well as philosophers. Vedāntins try to fathom it with the help of certain analogies. Some of them are as follows:

The world is a dream dreamt by *ātmā*. Dream has no existence apart from the dreamer. Once the dreamer awakens, the dream disappears in him.

The world remained as *vāsanā*s in *ātmā*. Like a magician, it brought those *vāsanā*s out of itself creating the illusory appearance of the world.

A tree remains hidden, potent in its seed. Likewise, the world remained potent in *ātmā*. Its own vital urge brought it forth, forming the world.

A skilled and talented artist gives shape to some imagery that gets formulated in his mind. It is the artist's mind that finds expression as the art-work. *Ātmā* is the artist whose work is the world.

In their highest state of attainment, *yogī*s are at times seen by many to possess certain supernatural powers. These attainments are really the work of nature (*prakṛti*) inherent in them. Likewise is the world's emanation from the *prakṛti* inherent in *ātmā*.

Ātmā remains unperceived, and the world alone is perceived as an object. *Avidyā* (ignorance of the real and projection of the unreal) makes the unreal world appear as real. The world is sometimes pleasurable, but mostly painful. Evils of life are not attributable to any source other than *ātmā*. The miserable and terrible situations that arise in life are also *ātmā*'s own self-manifestation. Good and evil are human conceptions. In *prakṛti*'s perception, nothing is good and nothing is bad.

For a man asleep, the world is non-existent. For all intents and purposes, he himself is non-existent. All emerge and appear as the world when he wakes up. Likewise, instantaneous is the creation of the world from *ātmā*. It is no gradual creation. This notion of instantaneous creation is known as *yugapat sṛṣṭi*, as against the concept of gradual creation or *krama-sṛṣṭi*, that evolutionists hold.

The one, causal Substance alone is Real. Then what about the apparent existence of the world? It is *vivarta*, illusory appearance. The causal reality, without undergoing any intrinsic change, assumes the form of effects, just as water in the ocean assumes the form of waves. Such a phenomenon is called *vivarta*. No creation as such of the world thus takes place. This idea is known as *ajāta-vāda* (the theory of no-creation).

That Birth and Death are Unreal

How birth and death are unreal is demonstrated by the Guru in a purely logical way:

Take the case of an event of birth taking place. It happens to an individual. Does the individual exist at the moment the birth takes place? No, because someone already existing needs no birth; birth should be the coming into being of a new being. Was he existing before the event? Definitely no. Does he exist after birth? No, because the one whom we see as existing is not *the one being born*, but is *one supposedly already born*. Where does then the one who is being born exist? Not in the present, not in the past, not in the future. That means, the one who is being born (*janmi*) does not exist at any time. Then evidently there is no birth as well.

"All this is true with death as well. Then what is that we call birth and death? All is but the mysterious way of *cit* or *aṟivu* manifesting itself".

To sum up, the *being* of *ātmā* contains within itself the infinite potential for the *becoming* of the world. That potential gives birth to everything from within *ātmā*. It results in the appearance of everything — the qualified and qualities, the gross and subtle, mind and matter, cause and effect, pain and pleasure. Such dualities, remaining inseparable, constitute what we call *śarīra* or the body, literally 'that which perishes'. Whatever we can measure and ascertain with the help of *pramāṇa* (valid means of knowledge) forms part of this unreal. The real *ātmā* always remains imperceptible and therefore unmeasured. Such unreal apparent forms are known as *bhāvas*, and the one Substance is *ātmā, sat*. The world, in short, is the ceaseless flow of *bhāvas* that arise in the one *sat*.

Why the World Continues to be Perceived

That the world is unreal, has become evident from many points of view, and we are fully convinced of it. Then the question arises: why is it that the world continues to be perceived as existing as was seen before becoming convinced of its unreality?

What is it that you really see? Is it the self-manifesting *ātmā*, or is it the world as such? If the former is the case, then the question does not arise at all, for you do not see the world. In the latter case, you are still caught in the snare of *avidyā*.

In other words, even when you mistake what you see as the world, it really is *ātmā*'s self-manifestation. You don't see it as *ātmā* only because of the *avidyā* in you. Free yourself from its strong clutch. Then you will no longer see the world. In and through all the appearance and disappearance of everything, you will see only *ātmā* existing and thriving.

The *Why* of the World

Why should *ātmā* undergo the mysterious process of emanating the world from itself? Why can't it remain just *ātmā*?

Take the case of a small child. It plays with everything it comes across. It creates many things out of even mere mud, and destroys them immediately. The child enjoys doing so. This joy is that of seeing all the creative potentials hidden within being brought out. Everyone does the same though unconsciously. The same is true with *ātmā* too.

Sat, in its capacity of being *cit* in essence, has in it the urge to give expression to its own hidden potentials. Thus, it clears the path to the actualisation of its own *ānanda* content, which we call its self-enjoyment. The net result is the appearance of the world. This is the connotation of the concept, 'This world is but a sport (*līlā*) of God'.

We begin our search from what appears before us, the world. Now we see all the worlds as having become sublimated as or reduced to one *ātmā* or *aṟivu*. This is a sort of ascending part of our search.

Seen from the sublimest and the highest level of one *ātmā*, everything we see as the world below is nothing but one *ātmā* variously become manifest. At this stage of our speculation we descend from *ātmā* to the world.

In this latter perspective we see the *aṟivu* itself as branching into two: the subjective world and the objective world. They, like a two-branched wild creeper in bloom, forms the world. This creeper has a tree to support it, but is made invisible by the overgrowth of the creeper itself. This tree is called *māyā*.

10

Māyā

Asking impossible questions and insisting on getting them definitely answered is one of the many human weaknesses, an outcome, so to say, of man's divine gift of an enquiring mind. For example, how does a tiny seed keep within it a huge tree of the future? No one can answer this question with any definiteness. Similar are some of the basic questions concerning life.

How does the one Reality become many? How does it divide itself into mind and matter? How can pure Consciousness (*aṟivu*) assume the form of gross and inert objects like rock and metal? In Vedānta, the impossibility of answering all such basic questions is put under the cover of the blanket term *māyā*. Though it gives the impression of having given some explanation, really it explains nothing. Those who do not insist on getting a conclusive definite answer would prefer to remain satisfied, thinking, 'All this is just a *līlā* of God'. For the reason that *māyā* is no answer to such questions, its well-accepted definition is:

na vidyate yā sā māyā[1]

That which has no existence is *māyā*.

The Undefinable

For the satisfaction of those who do not become content unless they get a definite answer to all questions, the concept of *māyā* is introduced as a *śakti* (an indomitable potential) inherent in *ātmā* or *īśvara*. Though we know nothing about this *śakti*, having been taught nothing about it, the word creates the impression in us of having got an answer.

1. Narayana Guru, *op. cit.*, *Darśana-Mālā*, Verse IV. 1.

No school of Vedānta can dispense with this *māyā* concept for the reason that an element of mystery lurks in the Real. The *māyā* conceived by all admits mystery at one level of thinking or another, yet one's *māyā* concept is ridiculed by another. They differ only in respect of the level at which the door is opened to let the mystery in.[2] And, providing room for mystery in philosophical thinking is no anathema to Indian philosophers. They even admit that the greatest of all mysteries is the Reality we are in search of.

Māyā, thus, is a blanket term to signify all that is inexplicable in Reality, and therefore is undefinable. It simply tells us that there is a mystery in what we perceive. Therefore, it is thought that *māyā*'s presence is to be inferred from its effects (*kāryānumeyā*).

Though negatively defined by Narayana Guru as 'that which has no existene', the concept of *māyā* is vividly portrayed by him in Verse 51 of *Ātmopadeśa Śatakam,* with the help of the poetical imagery of the creeper we have just seen as the last chapter concluded. A tree supports the overgrowth of the two-branched creeper, the very same overgrowth making the tree invisible. Without its invisible support the creeper cannot grow. Likewise is the *māyā*-tree. Without admitting an invisible mystery lurking behind the well-structured world, it can never be conceived, nor can it be explained. The Guru, therefore, supplements the above negative definition thus:

> Because of it arise the *vidyā-avidyā* duality, the *parā-aparā* duality, and such factors as *tamas, pradhāna, prakṛti* and so on.[3]

The Effects of *Māyā*

Māyā, we have already seen, is a mysterious principle that could only be inferred from its effects. What are those effects? All the apparent dualities — such as one-many, subject-object, cause-effect, *vidyā-avidyā, parā-aparā* — are its effects. For Narayana Guru *avidyā* also is thus an effect of *māyā,* although with Śaṅkara it is more or less a synonym for *māyā*. Put otherwise, the knowing function of

2. For details, see: *Vedanta up to Narayana Guru* by the present author.
3. Narayana Guru, *op. cit., Darśana-Mālā,* Verse IV. 1.

Consciousness become manifest, appears both as *vidyā* and *avidyā*. Narayana Guru, though an avowed proponent of Śaṅkara's philosophy of Advaita, deviates slightly thus in this detail.

Yet another case where the Guru deviates from the traditional line of the Advaita School is in respect of the concepts of *jīvātmā* (individual self) and *paramātmā* (Supreme Self). This dual concept never finds place anywhere in the writings of the Guru, though their place in the philosophy of Śaṅkara is crucial. It may be of interest to note that these two terms do not appear anywhere in the major Upaniṣads nor in the *Bhagavad Gītā*. Of course, the word *paramātmā* appears, but not as the counterpart of *jīvātmā*. Their origin is the Nyāya system. Why is it so? What is Real is *ātmā* alone, or *Brahman* alone; it is as an effect of *māyā* inherent in *ātmā* or *Brahman* that the Real appears to be having these two, mutually-exclusive facets, creating the impression that they really exist.

So is the duality, *para-Brahman* and *apara-Brahman*. Śaṅkara conceives *Brahman* appearing as the world as *apara-Brahman* (non-transcendental *Brahman*), and *Brahman*, as abstract substance, as *para-Brahman* (transcendental *Brahman*). These two, in the Guru's perception, do not exist separately except in our imagination. Just as gold content and ornament-forms do not exist separately, the all-underlying Reality and the apparent, changeful world do not really exist separately and are never separable. In other words, differentiating *para-Brahman* and *apara-Brahman* is also an effect of *māyā*. This effect of *māyā* is seen by the Guru, not as related to what really exists, but as relevant to the context of the one, unconditioned Consciousness becoming conditioned and assuming the forms of distinct human experiences. He defines the *parā* as:

> That because of which emanate such subtle organs as senses, mind, intellect, the five vital breaths, from the one *ātmā* that is *cit* in essence, is called *parā*.[4]

> And, conditioned by such subtle organs, the *ātmā*, *cit* in essence, becomes deluded, and thus feels, 'I am happy', 'I am unhappy' and the like, all because of its own *māyā*.

4. Narayana Guru, *op. cit.*, *Darśana-Mālā*: Verses IV. 5, 6.

Then the *aparā-māyā* or the *aparā* aspect of *prakṛti*, is defined thus:

> That because of which emanate all the sense-objects that constitute the gross world, is called *aparā*. It, in essence, is the concretisation of the *ātmā's* intentions (*adhyātma-sthūla-saṁkalpanā-mayī*).[5]

All the gross entities that form the world thus, in the Guru's perception, are nothing more than the intentions of *ātmā* or *aṟivu* become concretised.

How is it that our consciousness is in a constantly altering state, oscillating between waking and sleeping states, in such a way that when in one state the other remains absent? It is because of *māyā*.

In the ocean of Consciousness is latent this expert-for-everything *māyā*. It causes the emergence of endless effects along with the distinguishing features of each. Spatiality and temporality, too, are caused by the same *māyā*.

How all that constitutes the world, made distinct by *māyā* in *ātmā*, still remains integrally whole and inseparable, is depicted by the Guru, again resorting to the ocean analogy, but in a more poetic way, thus:

> The self-activating principle (*prakṛti*) is the water of the ocean; individual bodies, the foam; the ocean itself, *ātmā*; the always-swaying individuated 'I'-sense, the series of waves; the wisdom that blossoms within is the pearls that grow in the depths of the ocean; the wisdom itself is the immortal bliss that each relishes.[6]

The Source

In short, *māyā* is the root cause of the appearence and experience of the world. This *māyā*, along with its effects, is unreal and has no existence apart from *māyin*, the abode of *māyā*. This *māyin* is none other than *ātmā* or *aṟivu*.

---

5. Narayana Guru, *op. cit.*, *Darśana-Mālā*: Verse IV. 7.
6. Narayana Guru, *op. cit.*, *Ātmopadeśa Śatakam*: Verse 75.

If *māyā*, is the cause of the world, is it the material cause or the efficient cause? Neither. Both these causes, we know, are *Brahman* or *ātmā*. *Māyā*, then, is the mysterious cause that differentiates cause and effect.

Māyā being the cause of the world is meaningful in an epistemological context — the context of knowledge going wrong, in not seeing the real and mistaking the unreal (the world) as the real. This ignorance creates the impression that the world exists; in its absence no world is there. In this sense alone, *māyā* is the source of the world; *māyā* is not the ontological cause of the world.

A Veil (*Āvaraṇa*)

Cause and effect do not exist separate. Their separateness is merely imaginary, as in the case of gold and ornament. Yet we conceive of them as separate. Even then their existence continues unaffected, as inseparably one. That functional element in our consciousness which makes this imaginary separateness of cause and effect, of *ātmā* and world, is nothing other than *māyā*.

When we see an ornament, it is as if the gold recedes from our view. Of course the jeweller sees all ornaments as gold when he weighs them and fixes their price. Likewise, to the degree that we see the world, to that degree the *ātmā*-content gets concealed. This concealment of what is real by its own assumed form is known as *āvaraṇa* (veil). In other words, the world as an *āvaraṇa*, conceals *ātmā*. The same *āvaraṇa* of my individuated form conceals my being *ātmā*. The same creates the impression, 'I and consciousness are two', 'I am the possessor of consciousness'. When this *āvaraṇa* is removed, I and consciousness become revealed to be non-dual, the world and *ātmā* to be non-dual. So what we are looking for is the way to remove this veil.

Transcending *Māyā*

Removal of this veil requires the penetrative eye of seeing one *ātmā* in all that appears as many. Knowing *māyā* that causes this veil and thus removing it, is impossible for the reason that it is a non-existent mystery. Anything mysterious is never understood.

Yet a discriminating mind can win over and transcend it. How? By directing the enquiring mind's attention towards itself, towards the substance that assumes the form of that mind. Then that mind finds itself, the enquirer finds oneself, to be what one was till then seeking, in essence. One realises, 'I am That'. Then the mind or the enquirer finds no more veil there, no more *māyā* there. Transcending *māyā*, thus, is not a process of positively kicking it out; but on seeing the *ātmā* that oneself is, *māyā* is found to have vanished. Thus, it is a negative way. *Māyā* is something negative; its elimination also has to be a negative process. But this is possible only to discriminative minds gifted with intuitive penetration and wilfulness as we saw earlier in Chapter 5.

An overall picture of *māyā*, its effects, and the freedom from it, is given by the Guru in Verse 6 of his universal prayer *Daivadaśakam*. As addressed to *ātmā* or *aṟivu* conceived as God, he says:

> You are *māyā*; you are the wielder of *māyā*; you are the one who enjoys wielding *māyā*; you indeed are the one who wipes out *māyā* and bestows us with *sāyujya* (the final absorption into the one.)[7]

To clarify it: *aṟivu* or Consciousness (conceived in the verse as God) has in it the negative potential of knowing Reality wrongly; it is *māyā*. It exists in *aṟivu*; it is wielded by *aṟivu*. Unless this *māyā* is there in *aṟivu*, there will be no unfolding of *sat-cit-ānanda*, no experiencing, no enjoying; in short, no life at all. Because of *māyā*, *aṟivu* enjoys itself by becoming the world, by becoming life. *Aṟivu* thus is the wielder of *māyā* and the enjoyer of it as well. The very same *aṟivu*, functioning as the enquiring mind, frees us from the illusion created by *māyā* and thereby removes the veil as well. *Aṟivu* knowing itself and the removal of the veil are like two sides of one coin. It results not only in the revealing of the Real, but also in the seeker becoming merged in the Real. This final stage is called *sāyujya*.

---

7. Narayana Guru, *op. cit.*, *Daivadaśakam*: Verse 6.

11

Ātmā's Self-Manifestaton as 'the Known'

We have now seen that *ātmā* is the one, all-underlying Reality and is *cit* or *aṟivu* (Consciousness) in essence. In other words, *cit* itself, undergoing no intrinsic change, manifests itself as everything. This self-manifestation of *ātmā* has two apparent sides — the subjective and the objective worlds. That is to say, the world of 'knowledge' is *cit* become manifest, and the world of 'the known' also is so.

Consciousness is effulgence in essence. Having become conditioned and shining as a specific conscious experience is known as *bhāna*, literally 'to become luminous'. How this *bhāna* is structured to give the appearance of the world, is represented in more than one way by the Guru himself in different contexts. Chapter V of the *Darśana-Mālā* gives a detailed picture of it like this:

Bhāna is any specifiable aspect of the shining process incessantly happening in *cit*. On the one side, it shines forth inwardly as subjective experiences forming the world of mental images, the world of 'knowledge'. On the other side, it shines forth outwardly as the objective world, the world of 'the known'. Let us now focus our attention on the latter, reserving the former for the next chapter.

'The Known'

'The known' we refer to here does not exclude subjective factors imaginable, thinkable and conceivable, for they too become objects of knowledge.

The *bhāna* of *cit* has two facets: *sāmānya-bhāna* (generic shining forth) and *viśeṣa-bhāna* (specific shining forth — see examples given on pages 56, 57). Also, every *bhāna* depends on something, yet another manifest form of the same *cit*. This factor is called *bhānāśraya* (that on which *bhāna* depends). For example, consciousness shining forth specifically as the objective experience of a rose depends on the object called 'rose'. Here 'rose' is the *bhānāśraya* of the 'rose'-experience. There should thus be a *sāmānya-bhānāśraya* (dependent on which a generic experience shines forth), and a *viśeṣa-bhānāśraya* (dependent on which a specific experience shines forth). This much could well be charted out as follows:

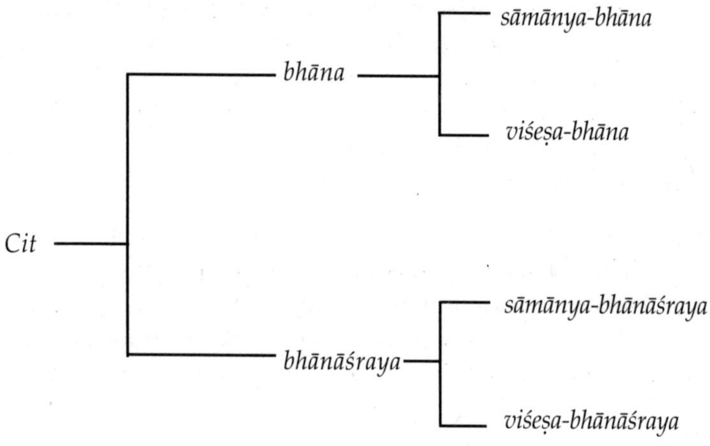

***Fig.* 1**

Bhānas Differentiated

Such conditioned shining forth of *cit* as objective experience is classifiable as four:

1. *sthūla-bhāna* — shining forth of *cit* as gross objective experience.
2. *sūkṣma-bhāna* — shining forth of *cit* as subtle objective experience.
3. *kāraṇa-bhāna* — shining forth of *cit* as causal objective experience.

4. *turīya-bhāna* — shining forth of *cit* as the fourth state of mystical union.

Each of these four modes of *bhāna* has a corresponding generic (*sāmānya*) facet and a specific (*viśeṣa*) facet, with each facet having its own *bhānāśraya*.

They can be charted out thus:

1

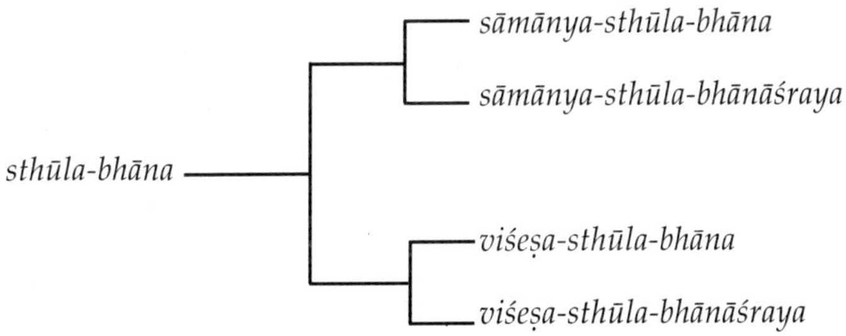

2

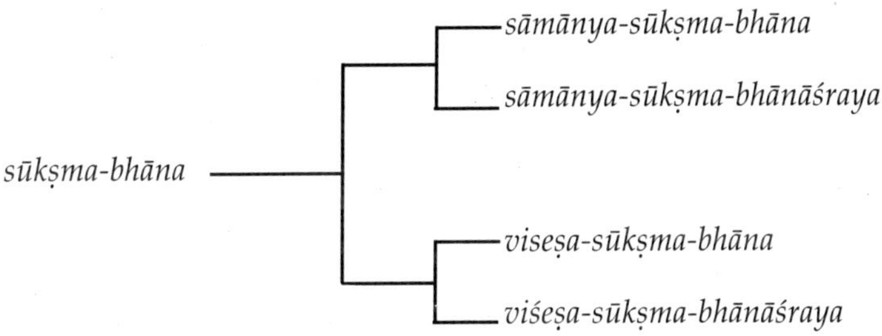

3

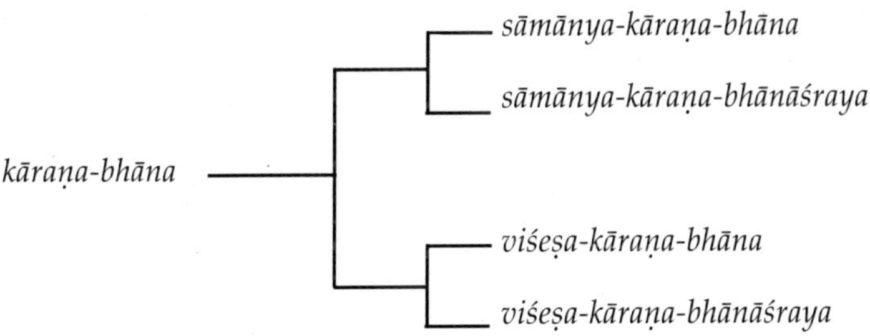

4

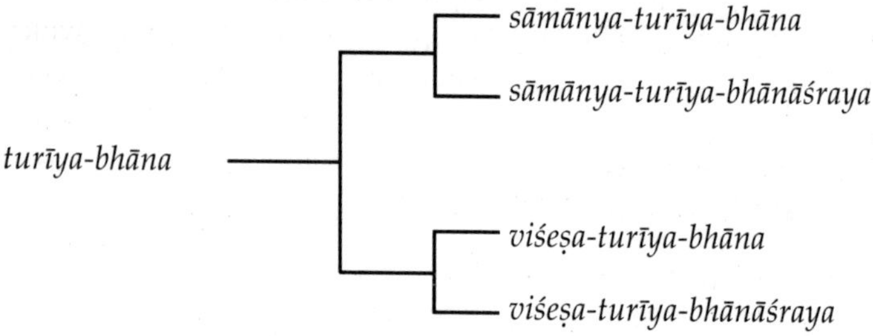

Explanation:

Sthūla-bhāna

I know I am now seated on a chair. Really it is my body that occupies the chair. Still I think I am sitting on the chair by identifying myself with this gross body of mine. In this case the knowledge I have of myself is dependent on the gross aspect of my being. Such experience that depends upon gross aspects of existence is called *sthūla-bhāna.* The experience, 'This is a pot', 'This is the world' and the like, are also *sthūla-bhāna*s. Consciousness thus becoming conditioned as the experience of a particular gross object is *sthūla-bhāna.*

Now take the example of the *sthūla-bhāna*, 'This is a pot'. Suppose you utter only the 'This' part of the sentence. It makes no specific sense, except creating a vague and general impression that you are going to say something about something. The word 'This' expects some other word or words to make its sense complete. Such potential of uttered words is known as *ākāṅkṣā*. Now you say, 'This is a pot'. Here 'is a pot' completes the sense and gives specificity to the vague and general expectation created by the word 'This'. Thus, the particular *bhāna* becomes a complete unit. Here, the 'This' part of the sentence taken apart is *sāmānya-sthūla-bhāna,* and the 'is a pot', *viśeṣa-sthūla-bhāna*. Likewise, the 'This-ness' in 'This' is the *sāmānya-sthūla-bhānāśraya* and the 'potness' in 'pot' the *viśeṣa-sthūla-bhānāśraya*.

Sūkṣma-bhāna

I know that I possess senses. I know their functions as well. With them I sense external gross objects. I know I have a mind with which I think, I imagine, I feel love and hatred and so on. That conditioning of consciousness because of which we become conscious of such subtle elements of our existence is called *sūkṣma-bhāna* for the reason that its dependence is on subtle factors like senses and mind.

Here also, in 'This is mind', the 'This' is *sāmānya-sūkṣma-bhāna* and 'is mind' *viśeṣa-sūkṣma-bhāna*. The respective *bhānāśrayas* are also to be distinguished as in the previous case.

Kāraṇa-bhāna

In deep sleep you are aware of nothing, even of your own existence. Only after waking up you say, 'I was simply unconscious (*ajñaḥ*) then'. The unconscious consciousness that you were at deep sleep, like a tree sleeping in its seed, is taken for granted to unfold itself as all conscious states; thus, it is causal, and hence its name *kāraṇa-bhāna* (shining forth of *cit* as causal experience). Again the 'I' part in this *bhāna* is *sāmānya-kāraṇa-bhāna*, and the 'was simply unconscious' part *viśeṣa-kāraṇa-bhāna*.

Turīya-bhāna

The final goal Vedānta aims at is the realisation 'I am *Brahman*' or 'I am *ātman*'. To the extent it is experience, it is a *bhāna* and is called *turīya-bhāna*. Again the 'I' part in 'I am *Brahman*', is *sāmānya-tūriya-bhāna* and the 'am *Brahman*' part, *viśeṣa-turīya-bhāna*.

Turīya, in traditional Vedāntic parlance, signifies the transcendental, ineffable state attained by great *yogins* and *jñānins*. Yet as much as it is conceived and verbally expressed, so much is it a *bhāna*. The pure transcendental enlightenment is something inconceivable and inexpressible. It is simply an experience of transparent brightness, all-engulfing. In silence alone can it find an expressionless expression.

Other than as any one of these *bhānas*, *ātmā* or *aṟivu* does not shine forth as such, as an object of knowledge. As is the eye invisible to itself, so is the *ātmā* never an object of experience to itself. Whatever the form of *bhāna* in which it assumes appearance as shining in a conditioned state, it never ceases to be *ātmā* either.

These four types of *bhāna*s could well be conceived as pertaining to an integral living system of consciousness functioning as follows:

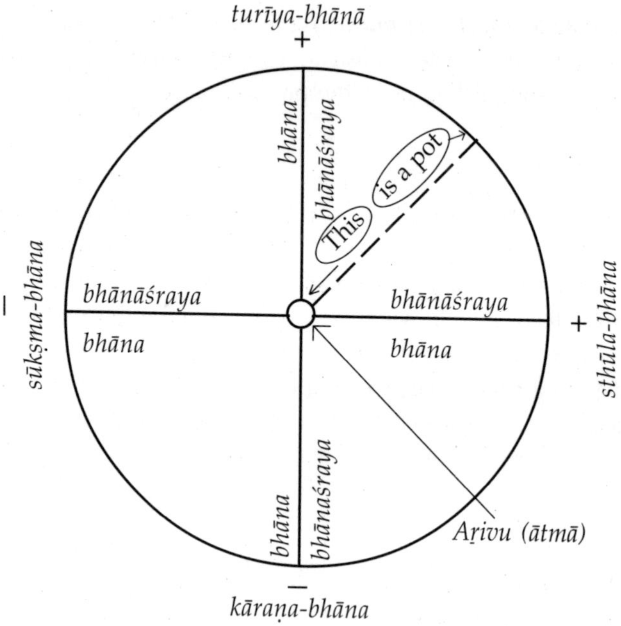

Fig. 3

Explanation:

The outer circle in this picture represents the overall field of the functional self-unfoldment of *ātmā*, the neutral centre standing for the non-dual *ātmā*. Horizontally and positively manifest, it becomes *sthūla-bhāna*; horizontally and negatively manifest, it becomes *sūkṣma-bhāna*; vertically and negatively manifest, it is *kāraṇa-bhāna*; vertically and positively manifest, it is *turīya-bhāna*. Each manifest form has its own *bhāna* side and *bhānāśraya* side.

The dotted radial line stands for any particular event of *bhāna*, e.g., 'This is a pot'. Of this, 'This' relates the knowing experience to its core Reality and 'is a pot' to the peripheral world, giving it specificity. Every such event of experiencing involves two poles, one generic and the other specific.

This scheme of the *bhāna* of Consciousness appearing as the world, is an original contribution of the Guru to philosophy.

Another Schemc of Self-manifestation

Yet another scheme of *ātmā*'s self-unfoldment as subjective and objective worlds is given by the Guru himself in his work called *Aṟivu*.[1] The relevant portion of it is summarisable as follows:

> The *aṟivu* you seek is yourself. And itself, as it functions, assumes the form of 'the known'. 'The known', thus emerged, are of two kinds: the knowable and the unknowable. The latter type is not classifiable for the simple reason that it is not knowable. The former becomes subdivided into five sense objects, again because *aṟivu* is functional. These five knowable knowns, the one unknowable known, knowerhood, and knowledge knowing — these eight together constitute 'the known world'.
>
> The same one *aṟivu*, on the subjective side, becomes transfomed as five-fold sense-knowledges, the knowledge that there is an unknowable or that there are unknowables, the knowledge 'I am the knower', and knowledge of the event of knowing. These too are eight and they comprise the subjective world.

In fact, what the Guru puts emphasis on is not the exact number of the constituent factors nor the preciseness of the process in which the unfoldment takes place, but on the one-to-one correspondence between the subjective and objective counterparts of one *ātmā*'s self-manifestation. The exact process of this manifesting is a mystery; it

---

1. Narayana Guru, *op. cit.*, *Aṟivu*, Verses 12-15.

is *māyā*. The picture represented here, when put in the form of a chart, will look like this:

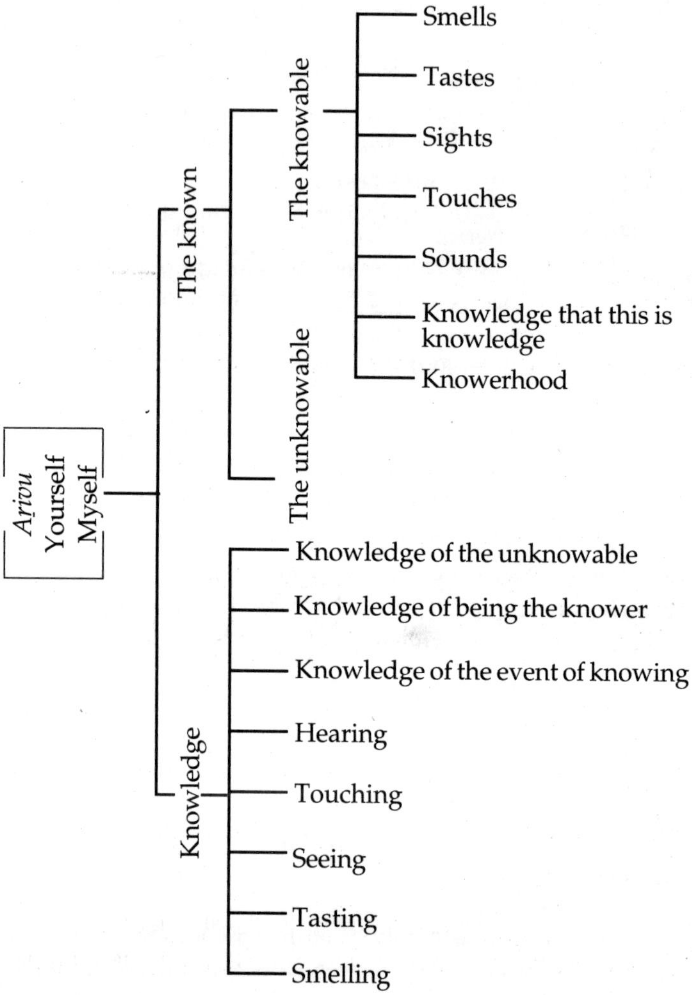

Fig. **4**

The Guru, concluding this analysis in the final verse of the work *Aṟivu*, reminds us: such constituent factors become meaningful only as you subject the function of *aṟivu* to analysis; otherwise it remains one undivided whole.

This is yet another new idea contributed by the Guru to Vedānta.

The Dialectics of Appearance and Reality

Though all these analytical studies help us have a clear understanding, really the one *aṟivu* (Consciousness) and its manifest forms (*bhāna*) do not exist one without the other. Similar to the inseparable oneness of gold and ornaments is their non-duality (*advaitata*). The eternal gold cannot exist without assuming some form that is necessarily transient. So too, the transient ornament-form cannot have being without gold that in essence is eternal. Similarly, the one eternal *aṟivu* does not exist without assuming the world-form analysable as above, and the ever-changing world cannot have being without *aṟivu* existing. Intuitively perceiving the inseparable oneness of the eternal Reality and the transient appearance is where non-dual perception (*advaita-darśana*) attains finality.

Speaking in terms of the diagram, the non-duality is experienced somewhat like this:

The effulgent core-dot becoming expanded as the infinite periphery-less circle, and becoming lost!

or

The infinite periphery converging and reducing to the effulgent transcendental core-dot, and becoming lost!

12

Epistemology

Epistemology is the philosophical study that investigates the origin, structure, method and validity of knowledge. Every school of philosophy has its own epistemology. What then is the epistemology of Vedānta? Seemingly it does not have such a separate section. Why?

What actually is the function we call 'knowing'? It is simply one of the many functional modes of one Consciousness or *aṟivu*, also called *ātmā* or *Brahman*. And this *aṟivu*, in its turn, is the one Substance that assumes the form of everything, and this *aṟivu* alone is the theme Vedānta deals with. Vedānta is itself thus epistemology or a study of Consciousness in its broadest sense; hence there is no relevance of a separate section for it in Vedānta.

Origin of Knowledge

Where does any particular knowledge orginate from? We have already seen that everything originates from the one *cit* or *aṟivu* and hence the origin of any specific knowledge also has to be the same *cit*.

In every event of knowing there is the coming together of two sides: the subject and object (*jñātā* and *jñeya*). What are they essentially? The subject is *cit* become manifest in a subtle form (*sūkṣma-bhāna*). In the case of an object, the same *cit* becomes manifest with a gross form (*sthūla-bhāna*). Of course, subjective modes of *cit* also sometimes become objects of knowledge. The subject and object thus are nothing but one *cit* shining forth in two different forms.

Cit never remains functionless because of the *karma* inherent in it. This *karma*-urge is there in every apparent form that emerges in the *cit* as well; both subject and object have it. This urge impels these two to get into contact with each other, in order that they could forgo their apparent differences and realise their essential oneness. In other words, subject forgoes its subjective conditionings and object its objective conditionings. The result is the two vanishing in their essential oneness of *cit*. This realisation of the essential oneness of subject and object is what we usually experience as specific knowledge (*viśeṣa-jñāna*). Though really it is an event of our realising the non-dual *ātmā* or *aṟivu*, we remain oblivious of it, just because of *avidyā*. The Guru, in Verse 48 of *Ātmopadesa Śatakam*, says:[1]

> *Ātmā*, confined in body, in its essential being, thinks of objects (of interest) as 'This is mine', or 'That is mine' and find identity with them, forgetting its embodiedness. Proper pondering on this makes anyone attain the final experiential non-dual oneness.

Every such event is comparable to rubbing together two pieces of hard wood to produce fire for a fire-sacrifice. The rubbing results in the emanation of fire that can consume the very two pieces of wood. Likewise, the coming together of subject and object results in the shining forth of the one *aṟivu* that consumes meanwhile both subject and object.

Methods of Knowledge

A method of enquiry, as we saw earlier in Chapter 2, can be either externally-oriented or internally-oriented. In the former case, the enquirer, the subject, looks for what is real in an object that exists externally. In the other, the enquirer, the subject, looks at oneself to know what one really is. The former method does not help us attain what is ultimately real, for the knowledge gained thus is always conditional and hence relative. The latter, on the other hand, is unconditional, hence absolutist, and therefore does help us attain

1. Narayana Guru, *op. cit.*, *Ātmopadeśa Śatakam*, Verse 48.

the Real. For this reason, it is the method Vedānta always relies on, as is clarified in the very first verse of the Guru's *Ātmopadeśa Śatakam*.

The *ṛṣi*s of yore were fully familiar with the details of *yoga-buddhi* or dialectical methodology as we have noticed in Chapter 3 earlier. Narayana Guru made use of this methodology with the precision becoming a *ṛṣi* of the Age of Science.

Validity of Knowledge

Now, how to determine whether the knowledge we gain is right or wrong? Some valid means of knowledge, known as *pramāṇa*s, are admitted by different schools of Indian thought. Perception (*pratyakṣa*), inference (*anumāna*), comparison (*upamāna*), presumption (*arthāpattī*), non-apprehension (*anupalabdhi*), and verbal testimony (*śruti, śabda* or *āgama*), are the six *prāmaṇa*s Vedānta recognises as valid. Darmaraja Adhvarindra, in his *Vedānta Paribhāṣā*, makes a detailed examination of these *prāmaṇa*s clarifying how they are acceptable. Narayana Guru defines only three of them (*pratyakṣa, anumāna* and *upamāna*) in the *Darśana-Mālā,* Verses VII. 6, 7 and 8. The validity of all these *pramāṇa*s is only in respect of the externally oriented knowledge. They never help you attain the self-knowledge Vedānta aims at. Being no object of any sense organ, the self is not knowable by perception. About something already perceived through sense-contact alone we can make some inference later. The self being a reality never perceived before with senses, it is not inferable either. For the same reason, *upamāna, arthāpatti* and *anupalabdhi* also do not help. The only indirectly helpful *pramāṇa* is *śabda* or verbal testimony, for it is the words of instruction the seeker hears or reads from an authority, a realised person. Such words, too, do not make the seeker enlightened straight away; he will have to ponder over them meditatively, no one knows how long, to get the hidden meanings of the words revealed. Hence Narayana Guru categorically asserts: 'How can any *pramāṇa* work with this unthinkable, ineffable enlightenment!'[2]

---

2. Narayana Guru, *op. cit.*, *Ātmopadeśa Śatakam*, Verse 94.

Logically, the inseparable oneness of the eternal *ātman* and the transient world is an impossibility; but the enlightened one realises how logic is of no utility in experiencing this oneness directly and intimately. An ornament is a transient form assumed by gold, an indestructible substance. If it felt at all, it could feel the presence of the eternal gold in itself. So, too, the enlightened one intimately feels the presence of the one *ātmā* as the Substance that fills his transient being.

We may come across thinkers who claim that what they can logically convince us of is the only right way of thinking, or the only way human mind functions properly. Another may question it and argue for yet another way of right thinking. Many may be such theories about the way mind functions and thinks. The reality is that the mind's functional capabalities are so infinite that no one can conceive or predict the exact way it works.

Structure of Knowledge

How consciousness, with a structural coherence and perfection of its own, unfolds itself as the world, we have examined in detail in the previous chapter. The same scheme is relevant with the structural pattern in which consciousness manifests itself as its knowing function as well. The Guru draws this picture in Verses 36 to 42 of *Ātmopadeśa Śatakam.* Verse 36 says:[3]

> Infinite is the way in which the knowing function becomes unfolded from the one consciousness; yet its entire range could well be classified into two: *sama* and *anya.*

We read in Verse 38:[4]

> The knowing function in which one perceives many realities is called *anya*, literally 'the other'; the knowing function in which Reality is perceived as one is called *sama* (the same).

---

3. Narayana Guru, *op. cit., Ātmopadeśa Śatakam*, Verse 36.
4. *Ibid.*, Verse 38.

Apparently, all worldly knowledge, all the externally-oriented objective knowledge, is of the former kind, and the internally-oriented knowledge in which knowledge knows itself is of the latter kind. Countless are the examples of knowledge that get configured as of the *anya* kind; but one knowledge alone is there to exemplify the *sama* kind.

Subjugating and winning over the *anya* kind of knowledge, though very difficult, is a prerequisite for reaching the *sama*. It will not be attainable unless one is endowed with an intuitively penetrative eye to see the infinite and the eternal, the appearance of the transient many notwithstanding.

Should the seeker, then, give up the *anya* and simply take into account the *sama*? No, on the other hand, one should realise that the one *aṟivu* unfolds itself as both kinds of knowledge, or else reductively see the two as meeting at one neutral *aṟivu*. That *aṟivu* is what the seeker is in essence, and in fact everything is in essence.

The *sama* and *anya* kinds of knowledge also, as in the case of *bhāna* of consciousness as the 'known world' seen in Chapter 11, each has a *sāmānya* side and a *viśeṣa* side. To cite an example: the knowledge 'This is a pot' is of the *anya* kind, and of it, the 'This' part is *sāmānya* and 'is a pot', *viśeṣa*. Both together give completeness to a unit of knowing, in this example, of knowing a pot. The place of 'pot' can be occupied by anything in this world. The 'This' will always be common with every such knowledge, and is given specificity by such as pot, tree, man, animal, and so on. This 'This' in other words, is the one from which the magic-like emanation of myriad specificities happens within Consciousness.

Knowing a pot is knowledge; knowing a tree is knowledge; knowing a man is yet another item of knowledge; and endless are such specific items of knowledge. Gone one more step deeper, we could very well say concerning any such specific knowledge, 'This is knowledge'. That means, all specific knowledge converges and reduces to 'This is knowledge'. It, in other words, is a statement true with any knowledge. In 'This is knowledge' also is there a *sāmānya* side and a *viśeṣa* side. As in the previous case, the 'This' signifies the *sāmānya* side, and 'is knowledge', the *viśeṣa* side.

A *Sādhanā*

'This is knowledge', thus is, the one all-inclusive knowledge we can conceive of. Now meditate on what the *sāmānya* 'This' connotes. It is that from which the specificity 'is knowledge', emanates. The more you try to get at it, the more it becomes elusive, incomprehensible, all-inclusive, to be short, mysterious. In fact, intuitively perceiving what this 'This' connotes is the ultimate goal Vedānta aims at. Here you get a clear path well defined by the Guru to direct your functional mind towards attaining the final goal. Such a methodical way of directing one's mind in search of the Real, is called *sādhanā* translatable as 'spiritual discipline'.

What, in short, is the kind of *sādhanā* Narayana Guru recommends to attain the final goal?

1. Let the seeking mind turn inwards and see for itself what substance assumed the form of the very seeking mind.

2. Train the mind to see all kinds of specific knowledge as just 'knowledge', and treat each as 'This is but just knowledge'. Turn your attention then to the specific part 'is knowledge' of the statement 'This is knowledge', and then retreat to the 'This' part of it. This 'This' is what assumes the specificity, 'is knowledge'. Your meditative search winds up in you getting lost in this 'This'. Then 'This' alone remains!

This 'This' is the *ātmā*; it is the *aṟivu*; it is *Brahman*. You are That! I am That!

This *sādhanā* is to be practised, of course, in view of what we saw earlier in Chapter 3.

This could also be diagramatically made easy to conceive as shown in the *fig*. 5.

A perfect parity between 'the world of the knowables' and 'the world of knowledge' is discernible in the structural details of both *figs*. 3 and 5.

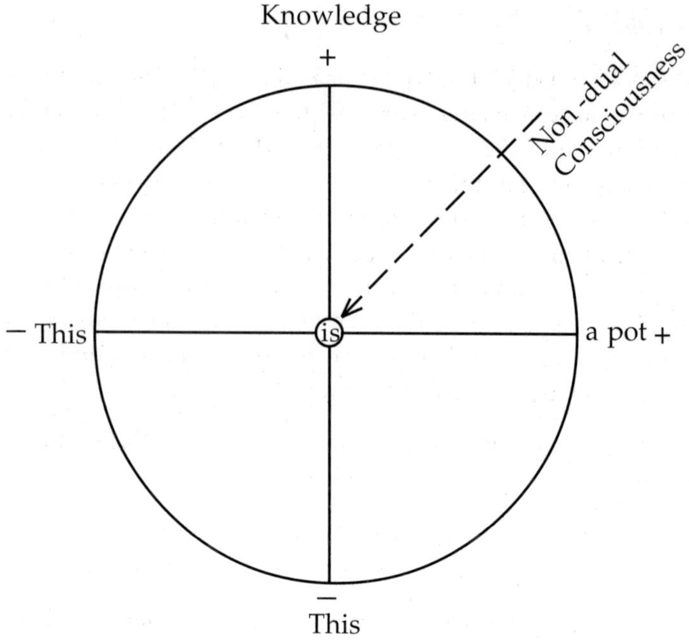

Fig. 5

Explanation:

The horizontal axis represents the *anya* kind of knowledge, of which 'This is a pot' is an example. The *sāmānya* part of it (This) is seen as the negative pole, and "a pot" the *viśeṣa* part, as the positive pole.

The vertical axis represents the *sama* kind of knowledge, of which the only example is 'This is knowledge'. Of it, 'This' is the vertical negative and 'knowledge', giving specificity to 'This', is its positive counterpart.

The neutral 'O' where the 'is' is, represents the non-dual Consciousness into which all manifestations are reduced.

This structural analysis and the *sādhanā* suggested is another contribution of the Guru to philosophy.

13

Sat-Cit-Ānanda

SAT-CIT-ĀNANDA is how *ātmā* or *Brahman* is defined, and realising oneself as *saccidānanda* is the final goal. Much has already been said on what *sat-cit-ānanda* means. Going into details would be endless, for the reason that endless is the way *saccidānanda* finds manifest expression. Let us now therefore simply tie some loose ends together by way of concluding this study.

Sat

Sat, as we know, means existence pure and simple, what really exists, the Reality. That of oneself is the most directly experienced of all existences. Your own apparent being is nothing but what is real in you become manifest. Your existence undeniably is as part of the existence of the total world; this world, too, is nothing but what is real in you become manifest. The Real does not and cannot exist without becoming manifest, and manifest forms do not exist without the unmanifest Real. This unmanifest Real is what we call *sat*, and the manifest form, *bhāva*. As the *Bhagavad Gītā* puts it in uniquivocal terms:[1]

> The unreal cannot assume manifest forms, and without assuming manifest forms the Real cannot exist either. A real philosopher (*tattva-darśin*) alone perceives what hides in between the two.

The manifest form (*bhāva*) of the Real (*sat*) is what we call the world. The Real is eternal, and all apparent forms transient. That the eternal

---

1. *Bhagavad Gītā, op. cit.,* Verse II. 16.

Real and the transient appearances remain inseparably one is a fact, though logically it is a contradiction. This inseparability could well be diagramatically clarified thus:

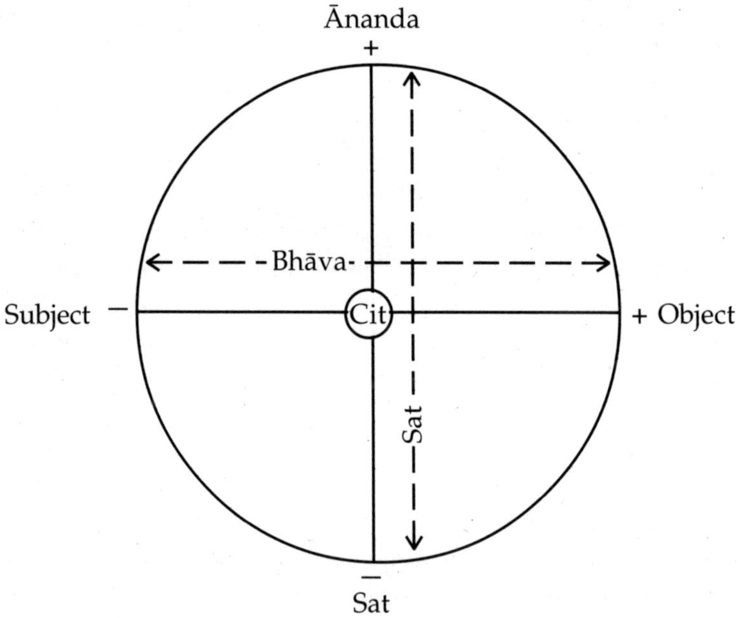

***Fig.* 6**

Explanation:

The horizontal axis stands for the world of appearances or of *bhāvas*, the negative pole representing the subjective side and the positive pole, the objective side. The vertical axis stands for *sat-cit-ānanda*, existentially considered *sat*.

The neutral point, neither vertical nor horizontal, neither positive nor negative, is where *sat* and *bhāva* meet. The circle around stands for the total world, and the central point for *sat* in its capacity as *cit*.

Cit or *arivu* thus concretised and self-unfolded, is the world. As the abstract Reality, it is unthinkable and ineffable, expressible only by silence.

The neutral point symbolises the non-dual inseparability of the world and *aṟivu*.

It is an everyday experience that the emerging and re-merger of apparent forms, really unreal, can never make what really exists unreal. The appearing or disappering of the ornament form does not make gold unreal. Every experience, we know, is of existence; no experience of non-existence is there. Having incessant experience means what is experienced has ceaseless existence; experience itself being existent. And experience, no doubt, is something that takes place in consciousness. The appearance of the world and experiencing it does not make the all-underlying *aṟivu* unreal.

Inherent within *sat* or rather *sat-cit-ānanda* is the infinite urge for self-unfoldment, called *viśva-vīrya* (cosmic creative urge). Endowed with this urge, *sat* is called *prakṛti*. The self-unfoldment of *prakṛti* results in the emerging of the world of dualities, the most primary being that of the subject and the object, called *ahanta* and *idanta* by the Guru. Other such dualities include *aṇu* and *akhaṇḍa* (the atomically small and the infinitely large), *sat* and *asat* or *asti* and *nāsti* (the real and the unreal), *kāraṇa* and *kārya* (cause and effect), *antaḥ* and *bahiḥ* (internal and external), *nitya* and *anitya* (eternal and transient), *bandha* and *mokṣa* (bondage and liberation), *vidyā* and *avidyā* (science and nescience), and the like. One feels oneself to be atomically small. According to Narayana Guru,[2] this infinitely small merges in the being of one infinite *aṟivu* or *cit*, and this merger ensures the plenitude of the infinitely large — a state inconceivable and inexpressible, but experientially very easy to attain. Such is the one *sat*.

Perceiving this one living *sat* alone in everything that appears as real and unreal, and finding one's own living existence merged in it, is how the attainment of the final goal becomes consummated.

Cit

Giving more importance to seeing the one all-underlying Reality as *cit*, *aṟivu* or Consciousness, is one of the peculiarities anyone can

2. Narayana Guru, *op. cit.*, *Ātmopadeśa Śatakam*, Verse 97.

notice in the philosophy of Narayana Guru. The present study till now also has been more or less an enquiry into how one *aṟivu* functions in many ways. It is not necessary to repeat it here.

Let us now, therefore, simply see how seeing the one Reality as *cit* resolves easily, or helps us avoid, many of the puzzles that have been forever tormenting philosophy in general as well as some puzzles peculiar to Advaita Vedānta.

1. How do the senses and mind, subtle in nature, get into contact with external objects, gross in nature, resulting in perception? This common sense problem has never been satisfactorily solved in a reasonable way by any philosophy or science. Narayana Guru's probable answer would be somewhat like this:

   Both subject and object are nothing but one *aṟivu* become manifest in two different modes, and therefore the two are really one in essence. The event of sense perception is simply that of the subtle and gross forms of appearance forgoing their conditioning factors — subtleness and grossness — and realising their intrinsic oneness.

2. Which orginated first, the chick or the egg? Logically this is a puzzle, but the Guru's philosophy enables us resolve it thus:

   The egg and the chick are nothing more than two successive stages in the beginningless and endless process of the creative self-unfoldment of one *aṟivu*. Seeing them related as cause and effect, because of *avidyā*, made of it a puzzle.

3. One of the major problems that torments modern scientists and philosophers alike is that of the origin of life from matter. The problem arises from the preconceived notion or rather the prejudice, that matter is the causal reality behind every natural phenomeon including life. This notion is not a scientifically proven conclusion, but is just a belief as blind as the belief that God created everything.

The solution to this conundrum derivable from the philosophy of Narayana Guru would be somewhat like this:

Matter and life are simply two different facets of the self-unfoldment of one *aṟivu*. Relating the two as cause and effect is meaningless. The only causal Substance is *aṟivu*, and it, because of the mysterious creative urge inherent in it, unfolds itself as both matter and life.

Closely associated to this problem is another one: whether matter abides in mind or is it the other way round. Here also the solution is almost the same: the relationship between mind and matter is not of one abiding in the other; the two, on the other hand, are simply the subtle and gross forms in which one *aṟivu* manifests itself simultaneously. Again, like the two sides of one coin, one does not appear without the other.

4. Seeing miracles is yet another phenomenon that has created many a godman of ordinary humans.

An enlightened one lives in complete identity with the whole, with the mysterious whole. This sense of identity makes the mysteriousness of the Real, the mysteriousness of the whole, his also. His life and activities also then become mysterious. He actually shows no miracles; only the unenlightened see miracles in him.

A *yogī*'s living, his activities, are all in the realm of the Real which is a mystery. His life will naturally look like a miracle to those who live in the world of appearances, in the world of the unreal, in the world of *avidyā*.

Many such miracles were seen in the life of Narayana Guru also; yet references to such hardly find place in his philosophical works, exept once. In the *Advaita Dīpikā*, while expounding the mysteriousness of the way the one *ātmā* or *aṟivu* assumes all the myriad forms of appearance, he compares it to a *yogī* assuming all forms even as he remains unchanged.[3] In his own words:

"In *ātmā* is there no I-sense;
It, like a *yogī*, because of *māyā*, sports in myriad ways."

A *yogī*, remaining unchanged in his firmness of the *yoga*-state, sports and enjoys assuming the myriad forms of appearance.

Such statements do not come from someone who had not had that sport and joy himself.

Miraculous events take place in the Real because of *māyā*, and this *māyā* is often compared to magic by the Guru. All the tricks and manipulations played by a magician are appreciated and enjoyed by spectators. Does the magician enjoy them himself? No. Why? Because he knows what he does. The spectators see them as miraculous simply because they do not know what the magician does. In other words, it is the spectators' ignorance that makes the show enjoyable.

Likewise, it is our ignorance of the Real that makes certain strange happenings miraculous. What we need then is to eradicate that ignorance, not worship the 'miraculous' phenomenon or the person in whom it is seen. Once ignorance is gone, one realises that the entire world and the life in it is a Great Miracle appearing in the Real! Nothing is impossible or improbable there. What we count as miracles ordinarily are nothing but minute particles of the Great Miracle called *aṟivu*, *ātmā* or *Brahman*.

The human mind is incapable of deciding what is possible in *prakṛti* and what is impossible, and to that extent deciding whether a phenomenon is natural or supernatural also is not possible. The reason is that human mind also is simply part of *prakṛti*'s miraculous self-manifestation. Ignorant of all this, we simply consider as natural whatever is familiar to us; all the unfamiliar seem mysterious to us. Really

3. Narayana Guru, *op. cit.*, *Advaita Dīpikā*, Verse 16.

everything in *prakṛti* is a mystery. For example, is it not a mystery that a vegetable seed sown produces vegetables from itself before long? We don't think of the miracle in it merely because it is an event we are quite familiar with.

5. We noticed at the beginning of this study that what philosophy does is enable us to comprehend three together: the perceiving 'I', the perceived world, and the transcendental Reality. The final realisation that one *aṟivu* alone exists and manifests itself as all, makes the three merge into one. The three will no longer be three then, but will be one *aṟivu* manifesting itself variously.

6. A problem arises when the ultimate Reality is thought of as *Brahman*: does such a *Brahman* really exist? Śaṅkara, while commenting on the *Brahma-Sūtras* of Bādarāyaṇa, strongly felt this difficulty. On the other hand, *ātmā* or self needs no such proof of existence; the most directly experienced, self-evident reality is of oneself, *aṟivu* or consciousness in essence. Knowing *ātmā* means knowing Reality.

7. Finally there is a way the great dictum *tat-tvam-asi* (You are That) could be properly understood.

   This has been a point of contention among different schools of Vedānta. (We have made a detailed comparison of it in our book *Vedānta up to Narayana Guru.*) Śaṅkara, whose line of thought Narayana Guru followed, found understanding the dictum in its literal sense very hard because the denotations of the words *tat* and *tvam* ('that' and 'you') are apparently opposite in nature. Hence, his preference to interpret the two words in their indirect sense (*lakṣaṇārtha*). No such difficulty is felt by Narayana Guru as he saw *tvam* (you) as consciousness in essence and *tat* (That), the Reality we are in search of, also consciousness in essence. Given that consciousness is one alone, the essential oneness of the *tat* and *tvam* is quite transparent. With the Guru, the two words denote only two opposite poles — the individuated and universal — of one Consciousness that alone exists and functions. The oneness of *tat* and *tvam* are like that of the wave and ocean.

Tat and *tvam* happen to the seen as two because of *avidyā*, and it is to be eradicated with *vidyā*. Both *vidyā* and *avidyā*, in their turn, are opposite facets of one Consciousness functioning, appearing to be different because of *māyā*. In other words, seeing one *aṟivu* alone both in *vidyā* and *avidyā* is the real, non-dual perception of *cit*.

Ānanda

Ānanda is not mere happiness. It is rather the norm that enables us to measure and discern each event as pleasurable or painful. Or else, it is the neutral value-sense that unfolds itself as our experiences of pleasure and pain.

This value-sense in each of us is an unsharable one; the pleasure and pain we feel are also so. One's experience of them can only be conjectured by others from the externally visible behaviour of one who feels pain and pleasure internally. The unsharable value-sense is part of our being and is eternally one with us. What we do externally is only a sign of what really is within.

What is the dearest of all for each of us? It is ourselves. This love for oneself is eternal whereas the apparent bodily existence is transient. That means, it is not the bodily existence we consider the dearest, but it is the essential, eternal Reality in us, the *ātmā* in us, that everyone loves.

To be engaged in efforts to attain something dear to us is natural and eternal with us. It shows, despite the transience of our bodily existence, the value-sense in us, in everyone, is beginningless and endless. And this eternal value-sense in all is what we call *ānanda*; it is unthinkable and non-dual. Eternally perceiving this non-dual *ānanda* alone in and through all the ups and downs of life is where we attain realisation of the non-dual *ānanda*, the Supreme *ānanda*, also known as *paramānanda*. This itself is the *mokṣa* (liberation) the Guru perceives.

Saccidānanda Experienced

The purely experiential merger of *sat, cit* and *ānanda* is given verbal expression to by the Guru in the concluding verse of the *Ātmopadeśa Śatakam*, thus:[4]

> I am neither 'that' nor 'this',
> Nor am I merely the meaning content of *sat* ;
> I am but *sat cit amṛta* (immortal bliss) —
> Having attained this transparency
> And becoming well-stabilised in it,
> With no preference for the real or the unreal,
> I should gently gently merge in the *SAT AUṀ* !

4. Narayana Guru, *op. cit.*, Verse 100.

14

The Science of Sciences

One of the Upaniṣads, *Muṇḍaka*, claims, what it teaches is *sarva-vidyā-pratiṣṭhā*, meaning, 'the one firm foundation of all sciences'. How can Vedānta claim to be so?

Vedānta is the science of *Brahman*, the science of *ātman*, the science of *arivu*, and the science of Consciousness. Innumerable are the ways in which this one Consciousness can unfold itself and find expression. All the arts, all the sciences, all the human disciplines are the one Consciousness manifesting itself in various ways. That means, one Consciousness underlies all branches of studies, which for convenience's sake, we call 'sciences'. If there is a science that concerns itself with this all-underlying Consciousness, then that science should be the foundation of all sciences as well. Vedānta, particularly as visualised by Narayana Guru, is nothing other than that science. It is thus the Science of all sciences.

To make it more explicit:

I am free to become involved in studying physics. My mind then functions as a physicist's mind. In the same way, I can become immersed in philosophical studies; then the very same mind works as a philosopher's mind. Likewise, many are the disciplines the one mind of mine can become interested in. If one Consciousness can function as the mind interested in all such disciplines, then a science that studies that one mind or Consciousness has to be the science that underlies all disciplines.

Consciousness growing and branching out as all sciences (represented symbolically by the verses of the Vedas) is compared in the *Bhagavad Gītā* to a huge banyan tree that grows upside down, rooted in the unknown high and branching downwards forming the ever-growing world of human disciplines. Certain downward-growing branches tend to seek to know the root; they thus bend upwards in their growth. Likewise, some roots grow down to become objects of study in the world here.

A Schematic Representation

Inconceivably abstract, the one Consciousness could well be diagramatically conceived as a point of no measurement. All the sciences, then, are countless rays radiating from this ever-scintillating point. All such sciences together could then be thought of as forming a circle of infinite magnitude. Each science, then, has a place in the circle somewhat like a radial line. One end of the line always touches the centre in its capacity as a particular way in which one Consciousness finds self-expression. Many spokes of a wheel are fitted into its hub. Likewise is the way all the various sciences find themselves well-fixed in one Consciousness. The other end of the radius, touching the periphery of the circle, as it were, is the specifiable field of interest of any particular science. The diagram will look like as shown as *fig*. 7.

The 'Universe' of Knowledge and Universities

We have in our universities many many fields of studies, one different from another, sometimes even inimical to one another. Our academicians remain completely oblivious of how all these studies find a common ground in the core-Consciousness, or how they never leave the bounds of the functional range of one Consciousness.

These universities supposedly are the centres meant to disseminate knowledge about everything in the universe. The word 'universe' is a combination of the Latin prefix *uni* (meaning 'one') and *verses* (that which has turned towards). To the 'universe' is then added the suffix *itat* (equivalent to *ity* in English), and thus was formed the word 'university'. The word thus suggests a state in which all turn towards one. Instead of understanding that all the various branches of knowledge turn towards the one Consciousness,

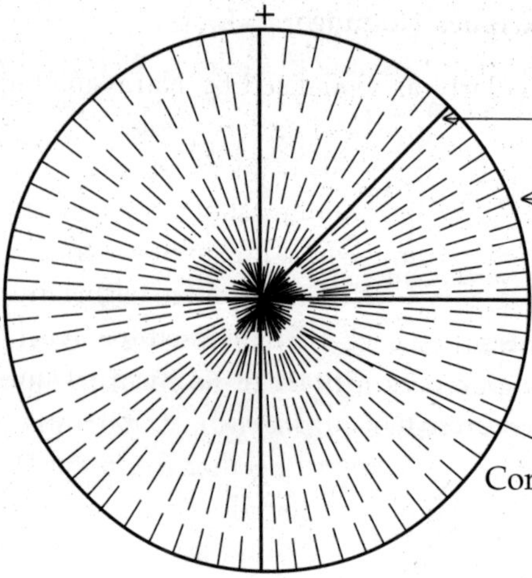

Fig. 7

what our universities do actually is making the study of all branches of enquiry centred at one administrative organisation. This lack of vision caused the diversification of human quest into unconnected fields of study.

This diversification went so far that the language of one discipline became foreign to another. This confusion of tongues is what the Biblical concept of Babelisation symbolises. The tower of Babel meant to touch heaven stands for unitive understanding, the awareness of the one core-Consciousness. The ill-effects of Babelisation have continued all through history in the form of disagreement between sciences, between religions, between nations, between states, between races, between philosophers. If two sciences find themselves opposing each other, it merely means, two rays emanating from one and the same point radiate in two opposite directions; it does not mean that intrinsically the rays are two in essence.

A Science that Excludes Nothing

In Vedānta, particularly as visualised by Narayana Guru, all the different sciences, even the seemingly opposite, become naturally integrated. It is not to be mistaken for an attempt to deliberately integrate all sciences. The field of interest of Vedānta is inconceivably vast for the reason that infinite is the possibility of the one Reality or *Brahman* becoming manifest. Within the range of this infinite field of interest there is room for each human discipline, each having its own value as a partial, miniature version of the one, all-encompassing *ānanda*-content of *Brahman*.

For this reason, Narayana Guru's philosophy cannot be considered one of the many schools of thought. On the other hand, it is a holistic vision of the Real, whereas the existing different schools of thought give stress to one or another aspect of what really exists. A student of any particular school or discipline, therefore, may find parallels in the Guru's words; but a single discipline never covers the entire range of existence as the Guru's vision does. For example, ideas basic to Śaivism, Vaiṣṇavism, Buddhism, Jainism, Nyāya, Vaiśeṣika, Sāṅkhya, Yoga, will be found in the Guru's works, but his vision transcends the bounds of all such 'isms'. So, too, notions acceptable to physicists, metaphysicists, biologists, psychologists and mystics, will be seen in the Guru's speculations, yet the Guru's philosophy is beyond all of them.

Logic and Mysticism

Every philosopher, consciously or otherwise, has leanings to two lines of thought — logic and mysticism. With Narayana Guru, both gain the same status in such a way that logical thinking ends up supporting mystical experience, and mysticism gains a scientific touch through logic. Each supports the other. For example, there exists a never-ending contention between creationists and evolutionists. The Guru, relying purely on logic, shows how everything is part of a great mystery. He says:

> Stationary state and moving state are contradictory to each other, and cannot be true with one object at the same time.

> So, too, contradictory are creation, sustenance and dissolution that supposedly take place simultaneously. These three really have no being. What appears as the earth and the like, therefore, are nothing more than mere words.[1]

Philosophers, scientists, and religionists are all in search of Reality. This Reality can never be more than one. Yet each thinker has his own theory or idea of the Real. To have more than one idea about one Reality doubtlessly means, those ideas do not represent the real Real. What the proponents of such ideas are after is establishing that what they logically prove represents the Real. In their over-enthusiasm *to prove* what the Real is, rather than *to realise* the Real, they often lose sight of the Real. All such contentions in no way affect what the Real is. The Guru, in a sarcastic tone, repudiates all such trends in his *Svānubhava-Gīti* in the form of a hymn addressed to Śiva or Paśupati thus:

> Not knowing who and what you are, O Pati, many here roam around in search of you. In their over-enthusiasm to argue for what they think of you, they become confounded and go around you, not recognising you seated right in front.[2]

The Guru's Vision

We have noticed that, with Narayana Guru, *Brahman, ātman, aṟivu*, God, are all synonymous. How he experientially and intuitively perceives this non-dual Reality is given expression to in different contexts of his works. For example, concluding one of his Tamil hymns to Śiva, called *Tevāram*, he says:

> In the plenitude of Existence, all that is unreal having become no obstruction, the notion of the primeval cause gone, the necessity of a mould in which the world is cast gone, the notion of effect gone, all conceptualisation of the Real gone, the non-dual meaning-content of *tat* (That) and

---

1. Narayana Guru, *op. cit., Ātmopadeśa Śatakam*, Verse 80.
2. *Ibid.*, Verse 93.

> *tvam* (you) that throws away all the sufferings, all the evils and also death — that transcendental Form is my God.[3]

Narayana Guru avowedly is an *advaitin* (non-dualist). Yet his non-dualism is not opposed to any other 'ism' like Viśiṣṭha Advaita of Rāmānuja, Dualism of Madhva, Buddhism, Jainism, Materialism, Idealism, Physics, Metaphysics, micro-cosmic vision and macro-cosmic vision. Still all such schools will find Narayana Guru's vision fully acceptable, each finding its own room in the all-inclusive mansion of its vision. His non-dualism is such that all the multiple 'isms' merge in the unitive vision of Reality.

3. Narayana Guru, *op. cit., Tevāra Patikam*, III.10.

PART TWO
APPLICATION

15

Ethics

Ethics is the branch of philosophy that deals with values relating to human conduct, with respect to the rightness and wrongness of certain actions and to the goodness and badness of the motives and ends of such actions.

How is Ethics related to philosophy proper? All quests, by nature, form part of human life, and human life only; philosophy is one among such. It is instrinsic to human nature to have value-sense and to make value-judgments. Philosophy being the quest for the ultimate meaning of life, value-sense and value-judgment can never be considered outside its purview. In the Vedāntic perspective and in the philosophy of Narayana Guru as well, more than an applied aspect of philosophy, it is in Ethics that the *ānanda* content of *ātmā* finds self-expression in actual human life.

Ethics in the West, till the end of the Dark Ages, was part of philosophy proper, as were religion and philosophy inseparable. The divorce of philosophy and religion, mainly impelled by the horrors the Inquisition, resulted also in the estrangement of value-science from philosophy proper. Yet no philosopher could turn a blind eye to value-sense; so inextricable is it from human nature. Each philosopher therefore had to think of Ethics in his own way with no religious leaning, and as a result it so happened that too many ethical theories arose and confounded humanity.

In the East

Different is the case with the East. Ethics and Metaphysics never became separated there. Philosophy, for Eastern philosophers, is aimed at ensuring happiness in life. Human happiness can never disregard value-sense either. Therefore, Ethics forms part of philosophy as the applied aspect of the wisdom it teaches.

The science of Ethics in India is known as *dharma-śāstra*, loosely translatable as the 'science of righteousness'. Yet the connotation of the word *dharma* is still deeper. Derived from the root *dhr̥*, to support, it means 'that which supports the entire living cosmic system'. The flow of this system is incomprehensible to human mind, for the very enquiring mind, along with the enquiry it makes, is a mere ripple that emerges in that grand flow. The best thing mind then can do, the only thing mind should do, is to find itself as inseparably one with the whole of the flow. Then an individual's flow of life becomes fully in line with, fully in harmony with, the cosmic system, also called *prakr̥ti*. Such a life is to be counted as fully in conformity with *dharma*. Otherwise, when the individual leads one's life taking cognizance only of one's own personal interests and gains, with no consideration for the total flow of life and for the life of others that form part of the total, then one's life is *adharma*-based.

'What is Good?', 'What is Evil?'

It is human action that is evaluated as moral or immoral. Actions that conform to rules of right conduct are considered moral, and immoral if otherwise. In other words, ethical principles applied in life form morality.

That all the actions (*karma*s) are *prakr̥ti*'s, not of any individual, we have noticed as early as in Chapter 8.

Prakr̥ti's actions as such are neither good nor bad; they are just *karma*s. It is only according to human evaluation based on human interests, personal as well as collective, that actions are counted good and bad. He who lives fully identified with *prakr̥ti* finds what he happens to do in life as *prakr̥ti*'s *karma*s, and thus amoral. Only he who thinks of himself as the doer of *karma*s worries about their goodness or badness. We can therefore safely say, a *jñānin*'s actions are amoral, and in that sense, good in an absolutist way. An *ajñānin*'s actions, on the other hand, could be either good or bad, moral or immoral, both having certain social conventions, all relativistic, for their basis.

For leading a morally perfect life, a *jñānin* needs no help of ethical codes; it happens so with him as a natural course. An *ajñānin*, on the other hand, finds himself incapable of doing so; so the best he can do is to follow the guidelines given by the enlightened. The collection of such guidelines is what is known as *dharma-śāstra*s in India. Though many in number, they generally do not directly teach whence those guidelines derive. Narayana Guru's philosophy is an exception in this respect. Many ethical directives can be found in his philosophical works, with their direct bearing on a well-conceived philosophical stand clarified.

The Search for a Norm

Any guideline given by a *jñānin* always applies a norm in deciding what is ethically sound and unsound in human life. Is there such a universally accepted and applicable norm existing? The search for it, particularly in the West, reveals, surprisingly enough, the fact that no such norm has either been applied or even discovered.

The enlightened man's moral teachings meant for the unenlightened will always have underlying them their enlightenment — the enlightenment that one *ātmā* alone appears as everything — as the guiding torch, though mostly left unsaid. Such teachings have implicit in them the fact that the effort made by everyone aims at revealing the *ānanda*-content of *ātmā*, of oneself, the one thing dearest to all. The difference between one and another is only with regard to the means or object that helps unfold the *ānanda*-content of *ātmā*. Clarifying this subtle point, Narayana Guru says:

> What is dearest to all is always one in kind; confusion arises only as to the pleasure-giving objects, such as, 'What I do like', 'What you do like', 'What the other does like'. Basically what is dearest to oneself is what is dearest to the other as well; this should always be remembered.[1]

---

1. Narayana Guru, *op. cit.*, *Ātmopadeśa Śatakam*, Verse 21.

The realisation that it is one *ātmā*, oneself, that unfolds itself as every being, every human being, gives human life a new directive in respect of man's conduct: that what ensures happiness to oneself should ensure the happiness of others as well. The Guru therefore says:

> What is dearest to the other is dearest to me as well; what is dearest to me is dearest to the other also. This is the basic guiding principle: The action meant for the good of one should ensure the good of others as well.[2]

Any action that helps ensure one's own happiness at the expense of the suffering of another, for sure, goes against the oneness of Reality, oneness of *ātmā*. By leading such an inconsiderate life, what one does really is making a hell of one's own life.

As a Science

Basically sciences are of two kinds: descriptive sciences and normative sciences. The former simply describes 'How things are', e.g., Physics is purely a descriptive science. Normative sciences teach us 'How things should be'. Ethics, if at all it is a science, is a normative one.

A normative science should have a norm, a scale to measure and decide which is commendable and which to be condemned. Ethics then should have a norm of its own to evaluate human conduct as morally sound and unsound.

Evaluating actions in terms of morality is a universal human urge, and Ethics thus is a discipline of universal significance. Does this universal science have a universal and unconditional norm? As we have seen, 'No' is the answer we usually get. Narayana Guru here comes forward with a new contribution of his own to philosophy — providing its branch of Ethics with an absolutist norm, based on the fundamental stand of his philosophy:

Any act that ensures one's own happiness and the happiness of everyone else at the same, is ethical. All other actions are unethical.

---

2. Narayana Guru, *op. cit.*, *Ātmopadeśa Śatakam*, Verse 22.

Inflicting sufferings on oneself to make sure that others are happy, in this perspetive, also is unethical.

The oneness of *ātmā*, *ānanda* in essence, is whence this norm derives.

Kindness and *Ahiṁsā*

Kindness to life and the noble habit of non-hurting (*ahiṁsā*) are yet other traits that spontaneously find place with those of the non-dual vision of Reality. In his work *Anukampā Daśakam* (Ten Verses on Compassion) the Guru counts kindness to beings as a dialectical outcome and counterpart of one's love for God. Without finding expression as compassion towards other beings, no love for God becomes fruitful, and unless one is endowed with love for God no worthwhile compassion finds place in life. All the great saints and prophets are visualised by the Guru as compassion-incarnates.

Killing other beings for eating is a practice prevailing almost everywhere among humans. Being a general practice in no way takes away from it the heinous kindlessness and lack of understanding of Reality it involves. Those who insist on living a principled life prefer to minimise the necessity of killing just to please the palates. At the very first verse of his *Jīvakāruṇya-Pañcakam* (Five Verses on Kindness to Life) the Guru says:

> Is it not to be rightly stated that all are brothers in *ātmā*? How can we, then, kill living beings mercilessly and eat them?[3]

I do not like to be killed myself. It is true with every living being. Then, how can I like to kill another being that really is myself appearing in a different form? Killing, in the modern consumer system, is done by someone else, not by the one who actually eats. The Guru puts his finger on this point and warns us: by eating meat you are making someone else kill living beings. Therefore eating meat is more sinful than the actual killing.

---

3. Narayana Guru, *op. cit.*, *Jīvakāruṇya-Pañcakam*, Verse 1.

The Guru was himself an embodiment of compassion and kindness. Not to hurt even an ant, as he underscored in the very first verse of his *Anukampā Daśakam,* was his ideal. At the other extreme, it was his compassion for the fellow human beings, especially for those trampled on by ill-conceived social customs and misconceived religious prejudices, that made him a formidable force, fully supported by his philosophical conviction, to effect a social awakening and upheaval particularly against casteism, hitherto unknown in history.

How the philosophy of Narayana Guru is a double-edged one, we have been stressing on from the very beginning of this study. If theoretical speculation and transparancy of vision together form one side of the coin that is his philosophy, the self-contentment one experiences uninterrupted in life, absolutely perfect morality, compassion, *ahiṁsā* and such other personal traits that outwardly become visible in practical life, comprise the other side. In other words, these two are the dialectical counterparts of the non-dualistic vision of Narayana Guru.

16

AESTHETICS

YET another study always thought of as a branch of philosophy is Aesthetics. What is Aesthetics? It is defined as the branch of philosophy that deals with such notions as the beautiful, the ugly, the sublime, the comic, etc., as applicable to fine arts, with a view to establishing the meaning and validity of critical judgments concerning works of art, and the principles underlying or justifying such judgments. In short, Aesthetics is the philosophy of art. Philosophy is the study of Reality. For a person, it is oneself that is the most directly experienced Reality; thus philosophy is the study of oneself. Sense of beauty being an essential part of human nature and human existence, Aesthetics also forms an inalienable part of philosophy.

Beauty: A Non-dual Experience

Our common notion is that beauty is an experience aroused by some object perceived by any of the five senses. How do certain objects have this peculiar characteristic? Vedānta teaches that the objects perceived and the subject who perceives, are nothing but one *ātmā* become manifest. We could better say as related to the context of Aesthetics, that it is the one *ānanda*-content of *ātmā* that unfolds itself as the enjoyed object, the enjoyer, the instruments of enjoyment such as the senses and mind, and even the act of enjoying. Narayana Guru portrays this picture in the *Ātmopadeśa Śatakam* thus:[1]

> One value-sense (*rati*) alone unfolds itself as I-sense, as sense-organs, as mental faculties and even as gross bodies. How

1. Narayana Guru, *op. cit.*, *Ātmopadeśa Śatakam*, Verse 70.

> can this process terminate as long as the knowing subject is thought of as separate? This is to be pondered on incessantly.

The self-unfoldment of *ātmā*, here of the *ānanda*-content of *ātmā*, happens because the *karma*-urge inherent in it becomes activated and thus *prakṛti* becomes apparent. This *prakṛti* causes the emerging of the enjoyer (*bhoktā*) on the one side, and on the other the emerging of all that is enjoyable. This is explicated by the Guru in Verse 81 of the above work. The Guru prefers to call the subjective enjoyer *ahanta* and all the objective enjoyables together *idanta*.

As we have seen, every enjoyment is an occasion in which the enjoyer forgoes his subjective conditioning, the enjoyed forgoes its objective conditioning, and the two realise back their essential oneness, that of *ātmā*. *Ātmā*'s self-unfoldment as the two provides also for the incessant infoldment of the two in the non-dual experience of joy. Such is the mysterious way of *ātmā*'s functioning.

What is the Beautiful?

Out of such myriads of appearances, some reveal the mystery of *ātman* or *Brahman* or the Absolute more directly than others. It is these we declare as beautiful. In short, it is the touch of the Absolute, the touch of the mystery of the Real, that makes something beauteous.

Some events or scenes are such that they immediately urge the evoking of the mystery of *ātman*; such scenes are beauteous. Many experiences of beauty are sex-related. Sex is part of the reproductive creativity of *prakṛti*, and hence the inevitable presence of beauty in sex.

What is Art?

Such situations of beauty are generally of two types: one, beauty of creation and two, beauty created. All that emerges as part of nature's inexorable flux comprises the former, for example, the beauty of a flower or the beauty of a landscape. Such situations created by humans comprise the latter. The human mind is so devised by *ātmā* that it is capable at will of perceiving even the mystery of *ātmā* in itself, and of re-creating situations that reveal that mystery. Such re-created mysteries are what we call art-works of originality.

How works of art are created, though mysterious, is familiar to at least a few. An artist feels his or her being filled with a mystery having a touch of the unfathomable. He or she then gives expression to it through the medium he or she is familiar with. What was within the artist and what finds expression as an art-work are really not two. What is within is virtual, and what is made perceptible outside is merely its own actualisation. The two in essence are one.

The World: A Work of Art

Comparable to this artistic creation is the creation of the world from and by the one Reality or *ātmā*. *Ātmā* is the artist and the world its art-work. *Ātman* feels itself filled with the self-creative potential called *karma* with an urge to give expression to it. This inner agony is called *tapas*. As a result of this *tapas*, *ātmā* undergoes transformation and thus emerges the world. Narayana Guru draws this picture clearly as follows:

> All this in the beginning was simply mind. Then, the Lord, like an artist, mysteriously enough, brought out this world as is seen here.[2]

The entire world then is an art-work of God, and its beauty is to be felt everywhere, not only in what is pleasing. Beauty then gains a new dimension, a vertical one, much different from the horizontal one in which beauty is seen only in that which is pleasing. Vertically perceived, the beauty of *ātmā* is to be visualised even in that which is seemingly ugly and disgusting. The horizontal kind of beauty-experience, in Sanskrit, is known as *lāvaṇya-anubhava* and the other *saundarya-anubhūti*.

Horizontally viewed, the experience of beauty is an enjoyer enjoying the enjoyable. What appears as the enjoyer and the enjoyed, is the one *ātmā* alone, to be more precise, the *ānanda*-content of *ātmā* alone. The event of enjoying, then, is the occasion in which both the

---

2. Narayana Guru, *op. cit.*, *Darśana-Mālā*, Verse I.5.

enjoyer and the enjoyed realise back their intrinsic oneness, as we saw earlier. Beauty, then, in essence, really is an experience of realising the *ānanda*-content of *ātmā* with its own manifest forms for instruments; but the enjoyer remains oblivious to this truth simply because of ignorance (*avidyā*). In other words, the ignorant, even when experiencing directly the non-dual *ānanda*-content of *ātmā*, remain unaware of doing so; instead, one thinks, one is enjoying a beautiful object.

Different is the case with the enlightened. Such a one too enjoys the beauty of objects as the ignorant does, but what an enlightened one experiences within will be the immediate vision of the *ānanda*-content of *ātmā* in terms of beauty. In both the beautiful and ugly, the enlightened, therefore, see only the variety of the unfoldment of one *ānanda*. Every such situation for him or her is an occasion for the immediate perception of the Absolute. Narayana Guru, in this sense, perceives the entire eight-fold world of enjoyment of Śiva as comparable to an epic poem conceived by a poetic genius. He says:

> The moon, the sun, the priest (of the fire-sacrifice called life, i.e., oneself) and the five basic manifest forms such as the earth — all these are but a mysterious magic of yours comparable to an epic poem of a poetic genius. Who does really know what kind of magic this is![3]

The beauty of an epic poem is not merely in the pleasing scenes portrayed in it. The most pleasing and the most tragic, the most sublime and the most common place — all these together make its reader appreciate the unforeseeable way the unfathomable makes itself manifest. This explains why tragedies that make the spectators weep as they leave the theatre, are well-recognised as works of sublime beauty.

Effusions of Ecstacy

Imbibing the absolute Beauty and giving verbal expression to it is what the Guru accomplishes in his mystical effusion *Svānubhava*

---

3. Narayana Guru, *op. cit.*, *Śiva Śatakam*, Verse 19.

Gīti (The Lyric of Revelation of the Realised Self). We quote below a few verses from it just to show how the feeling of absolute Beauty filled the being of the Guru all through his life:

> All this is pure Happiness indeed! The more contemplated on, the more it becomes the all-filling beauty unfolded! Seen closely, everything is a mere cage-like appearance that the one that underlies all and perceives all the worlds, transforms into.[4]

> O! the sweet sound that resounds and makes the basic elements such as fire, water and earth melt, blow up and become smoke-like. Lo and behold! it is the call of the jingling bells tied to your holy ankles that all the sacred scriptures try to reveal![5]

> O! the sacred call, O! the lustre of precious stones, O! the bee that comes flying whenever called, O! the neutral state into which go dust-like, the ever-changing fragrance, taste, sound and the like![6]

> Alas! I do know nothing! Splendid indeed is your magnificent sporting! O! the pure and original tree with the golden creeper entwined on one side![7]

> O! the original, pure tree! you alone are the protective shade for me. And your twin feet, the most beneficent fruits of yours — please adorn this head of mine with them for flowers. Lo and behold! are you not the sole great mountain that sways because of the heavy golden creeper? O! what a conjuring vision is this![8]

---

4. Narayana Guru, *op. cit., Svānubhava Gīti*, Verse 16.
5. *Ibid.*, Verse 32.
6. *Ibid.*, Verse 33.
7. *Ibid.*, Verse 81.
8. *Ibid.*, Verse 82.

The World as a Dance-Drama

The most noteworthy work of Narayana Guru as the effusion of aesthetic experience, is his *Kālī-Nāṭakam* (The Dance-Drama of Kālī, the Mother-Goddess). If a mathematical point (*bindu*) can magnify itself as the infinite cosmos, if one pure and abstract sound (*nāda*) can expand itself as the entire range of the world of words and sounds, then the one abstract Reality symbolised by Kālī, the Mother Goddess, in her performance of dance, assumes the form of all the worlds and all of life. A dancer, while performing, is movement-incarnate. Facial expressions and modes of acting appear in her or him in succession. These facial expressions are the enactment of variety of human feelings called *rasa*s. They are nine in number: *sṛṅgāram* (eroticism), *hāsyam* (humour), *karuṇam* (compassion), *raudram* (wrath or furiousness), *vīram* (heroism), *bhayānakam* (terror), *bībhatsam* (disgust), *adbhutam* (wonder), and *sāntam* (tranquillity). All these sentiments that we experience in our day-to-day life are perceived as part of the ever-changing facets of the Devī's dance performance that appears as the world. This dance-drama never ends; so, too, non-stop is the metrical style the Guru adopts to give expression to this unique experience: the metre is called *daṇḍaka*.

Emerging of Aesthetic Sentiments

Why does Devī perform this never-ending dance drama? Simply to enjoy herself, simply to feel the joy of seeing actualised for herself all the immense possibilities latent in Her own being. Devī, in other words, enjoys Her own mystery; *ātmā* enjoys its own mystery, and as a result arouses aesthetic feelings.

A poet, an artist, a musician, a dramatist, feels his own being filled with this mystery. This feeling in them finds expression as something that they create at that state of ecstacy, its nature, of course, decided by the medium of expression each is familiar with. That creation, a miniature version of the one immense Reality or Mystery, becomes an excellent art-work.

A spectator, a reader, a connoisseur, a listener, feels the same mystery within himself as he appreciates the art-work. To the extent the spectator fully imbibes the ecstatic feeling the artist or poet had while creating it, the art-work could be counted as having fulfilled its purpose, and such a piece becomes a universally-acclaimed art-work.

It is *ātmā* that creates it; it is *ātmā* that enjoys it; it is in *ātmā* that the enjoyment of the aesthetic sentiments happens. The sublimest of all beauty-experiences is that of one finding oneself fully merged in the beauty or *ānanda*-content of *ātmā*.

17

Casteism

Casteism is an interesting but perplexing social phenomenon peculiar to India, having much in common with the racism practised in some other parts of the world. Though supposed to have the support of religion, no canonical scripture of the first order of Hinduism subscribes to it as a social order. That science does not back it is self-evident. No philosophy worth the name also upholds it. Then how did it get into the Indian social fabric as an indelible stigma? No one knows clearly, despite the many theories sociologists and psychologists put forward. It is not our purpose to go into the details of its roots. Our concern here is the evil of inequality and exploitation it engenders across the entire spectrum of the Indian society, and the way Narayana Guru dealt with it.

Casteism is a sort of double-edged blade that cuts both ways. The discrimination involves a double favour for some, which they do not wish to forgo. It is a double loss for those who feel it as unfavourable: not only do they have to suffer the evil, but also they remain ignorant of doing so.

The second half of the nineteenth century witnessed the Age of Enlightenment at its full bloom. This enlightenment triggered the intelligent and sensible amongst the sufferers to rise against this injustice. Their voices started becoming pronounced. Exactly at that time the presence of Narayana Guru as an enlightened person began to be noticed, though this enlightenment meant something much different from the one the Age of Enlightenment embodies.

The Guru's enlightenment readily came out as a formidable support to the cause the other enlightenment made stand out. He thus became the focal point as a catalyst in the rebellion that was then gathering momentum. His sincerity and whole-heartedness towards this issue was so strong that at a certain occasion he even went so far as to say, if his devoted followers insisted on considering him an incarnation of God — they did so actually — they could do so only on condition that such a status was to be conferred on him as one who was born to annihilate the demon of casteism. The Guru's enlightenment that everything is but one *ātmā* become variously manifest, could not countenance any social discrimination among humans whether based on caste, religion, race or any other consideration.

Casteism and Racism

How are racism and casteism related? The former has for its basis mainly physical features and colour of the skin, whereas the latter is merely a long lingering psychological conditioning. This conditioning, with some groups, finds expression in the form of external signs like wearing sacred thread, and certain appendages to their names. Still racism sometimes comes in support of casteism.

Caste-discrimination forbids marriage between people of different caste-groups, and their cooking and dining together. Those of the lower caste were not to enter the houses of the upper caste people. Touching each other was considered to pollute those of the upper caste. In certain cases, even seeing each other, be it accidental, was counted as polluting. Even those of the lower caste had their own orthodoxy and sense of pollution and purity. Economically, those of the higher strata owned all landed properties and the others had to be satisfied with being workmen mainly in agriculture.

The Guru's Role

Many are the theories sociologists and psychologists put forth about the origin of this phenomenon. Whatever such theories, the undeniable fact is that the senseless caste-system and its discriminations existed and countinue to exist as a social actuality, somewhat like a bad dream. Awakening the dreamer is the best and direct way to save him from a nightmare. Likewise, what is required to save the social integrity from this nightmarish dream of casteism and its ill-effects, is awaking it from the bad dream it is in. And that is exactly what Narayana Guru did.

Affirmative Actions

Active upheavals and affirmative actions, though helpful to mitigate economic disparities to a certain extent, do not help get rid of casteism as a social evil. The positive actions the government resorts to are that of allowing special previleges such as free education, reservation in public jobs and democratic bodies and so on, to the under-privileged caste-groups. What actually happens as a result is that people of different castes organise themselves to gain strength to bargain for more and more such privileges and also to keep secure the ones already availed. Caste-identity eventually became more pronounced, more necessary, to the extent that it has a lot of say even in political power-sharing. What was intended to be cast away thus became all the more firmly rooted, a situation somewhat like shouting for silence in a noisy crowd which only makes the scene all the more noisy.

The Guru's Method

Helping those of the lower strata to rise upwards economically and even socially through such affirmative actions is apparently at the cost of they becoming more caste-minded. Securing equal opportunities for all for economic and social parity is one thing. Much different is the goal of doing away with caste-identity. While giving full moral support to achieve the former goal, what he put his finger pointedly on was the latter need that was of long-lasting, deep-rooted value. This was what the Guru intended while showing the model of rearing children of the under-privileged class in his own *āśrama*. The method he resorted to for this purpose was strictly scientific while being an outright application of his philosophy of oneness.

Casteism basically is an evil social phenomenon caused by ignorance, both of the orthodox and the heterodox, both of the privileged and the under-privileged. Altogether, it is something negative in nature. Anything negative can be eradicated only through a negative way.

The roots of casteism lie buried deeper than what social reforms can reach. *Jāti* is the Sanskrit word for caste. Literally it means 'birth', as in the word *jātaka* (that which is related to birth) meaning 'horoscope'. The word in biology means 'species' or 'kind', and sociologically, 'caste', 'tribe', 'class', 'race', 'lineage'.

Varṇa and *Jāti*

Varṇa is yet another word understood as much related to, often mixed up with *jāti*. *Varṇa*, literally meaning 'colour', is purely a psychological factor, not of any sociological bearing. It shows the mental nature of each individual person. Variety, always true with nature, is true with the characteristic traits of individual beings also. Such personal traits are classified in the *Bhagavad Gītā* as four — brāhmaṇa, kṣatriya, vaiśya, śūdra — and are admitted as pertaining to the Absolute, meaning it is just part of nature or *prakṛti*. One has to be fully aware, of what kind of person one is, to enable oneself to live a happy life in which one gets maximum opportunity to give expression to one's characteristic personal traits and thus find the joy of actualising oneself. The distinguishing marks of each *varṇa* are fully described in the last chapter of the *Gītā*. The *varṇa* concept of the *Gītā* thus does have nothing to do with any social hierarchical order.

There is, of course, a reference to *jāti-dharma* (the rightful duties of those who belong to a particular *jāti*) also in the *Gītā*, but only as a mention made by Arjuna while detailing the mental conflict he faces. This reference belongs rather to the *pūrvapakṣa* (anterior-position) part of the *Gītā* than to its teaching part. The issue is simply ignored by Kṛṣṇa in his real teaching, for it becomes quite irrelevant in the Absolutist wisdom he imparts.

Different is the case of *varṇa*s. The four *varṇa*s the author of the *Gītā* enunciates, have much in commom with the three types of people in an ideal state conceived by Plato in his *Republic*. They are administrators/philosophers, soldiers and producers. A fourth type of people called slaves were also there in Greece then, but they were not counted as forming part of the polity. Each type having engaged in jobs fit for them, with mutual cooperation, even as different parts of the body together form a perfect and whole living being, was the best social sytem Plato conceived.

Varṇa admittedly gained the status of social stratification later, especially after the advent of the epics, *purāṇa*s and *smṛti*s, all of them coming under the general title *smṛti*s, all secondary in their status as scriptures. *Manu-Smṛti* is wherein *varṇa* distinction gains a fully social dimension, causing much confusion and mixing up later with *jāti*. It may be noted that it is *varṇa*s that are described as castes in all the English dictionaries. Actually within the pale of a particular *jāti* can there be those having personal traits of any of the four *varṇa*s. Such persons, strictly according to the *jāti* concept, are considered as belonging only to that particular caste, regardless of their personal traits.

The Guru's Directives

Jāti is something that has no real existence, a baseless notion, a man-made social prejudice. The best way to eradicate this negative phenomenon has to be equally negative. The Guru therefore directed to ignore it conscientiously. Hence his directive, 'Do not ask caste, do not tell caste, do not think of caste'. A slow and steady educative process, this includes also doing away with references to caste in official records.

It is in the light of all this that we have to comprehend the connotations of his well-known dictum, 'One in kind, one in faith (religion), one in God is man'. The Guru does not deny outright *jāti* in the scientific sense of 'kind', or 'species'. Therefore, instead of denying *jāti* altogether, he says the entire human race belongs to one *jāti* or kind. No different *jāti*s are there, therefore, amongst human beings, but rather all belong to one *jāti*.

A species forms part of a genus, also called *jāti* in Sanskrit. If the scope of genus or *jāti* is broadened to its maximum, then we reach a genus that includes within its scope all the genera. This genus of all genera, virtually, is none other than God, *Brahman*, or *ātman*. The Guru's categorical assertion 'one in God' implies this.

Apart from being a catalyst in an all-round, slow and steady social awakening, by way of giving inspiration with proper philosophical and scientific backing, sometimes even by being personally present where some drastic correction was required, the Guru wrote two poems also on the theme of *jāti*. One shows the biological fact of the oneness of the human species and its application in social interaction. The other shows the deeper epistemological significance of *jāti*. In this latter sense, *jāti* denotes the unconscious categorisation into species, of anything we happen to comprehend. It forms part of the natural knowing function of consciousness. The already mentioned well-known dictum of the Guru appears as forming part of *Jāti Mīmāṁsā* also known as *Jāti-Nirṇayam* (Critique of Caste).

Jāti Mīmāṁsā

This small work of six verses, the first one in Sanskrit and the rest in Malayālam, shows how biologically and common sense-wise, caste as a social hierarchy is meaningless. Translated, it reads as follows:

1. Humanness marks the kind to which man belongs, even as bovinity that of cows. Viewed thus, brāhmaṇahood and the like are not so in this matter. Alas! no one is aware of this basic truth!

2. One in kind, one in faith, one in God is man. Of one source, of one form, difference therein is none.

3. From within a species alone is progeny produced. Human species, thoughtfully considered, therefore is of one kind alone.

4. From the human species is born brāhmaṇa as well as pariah. What difference is there amongst humans?

5. The great sage Parāśara of old was born of a pariah woman, and the sage (Vyāsa) who strung together the Vedic hymns was the son of a fisherwoman.

6. Is there the least of difference species-wise amongst human beings? Is it not true that only individual-wise there exists characteristic differences?[1]

The first verse suggests that brāhmaṇahood and its other pole pariahhood are superimposed on humans merely because of the confusion caused by ignorance. Such superimpositions are to be studiedly negated by the conscientious. Then the oneness of human species in all its purity becomes revealed.

Jāti-Lakṣaṇam (Kind Defined)

Jāti-Lakṣaṇam is the other work and it is of ten verses. Apart from giving emphasis to the biological oneness of human species, it goes also deeper into the philosophical or rather epistemological implications of the concept 'kind' or 'species'. Knowing something specifically is not possible without relying on genus and species even if unconsciously. For example, in the specific knowledge 'Man is a thinking animal', 'animal' is a generic term, and 'man' something specific that comes within the scope of what 'animal' denotes. In this case, thinking is the specifying attribute. At a subtler level, in the specific knowledge, 'This is a pot', 'this' is generic and 'pot' specific. Uttering the word 'this' alone creates only a general impression of going to say something about something. That impression gains specificity only when 'is a pot' is added. Streching this epistemological exigency out of its context and treating 'kind' to signify social stratification is what the perpetrators of casteism did.

The last three verses of the work, translated, read as follows:

8. Everything configured in the ocean of consciousness (*aṟivu*) has 'kind' for its mould. Waves appearing in rows are but the causal water in essence.

   ['Kind' or 'species' is the mould into which is cast what appears discernibly. 'Kind', in other words, does not exist apart from the one, all-underlying Reality, i.e., *aṟivu*.]

---

1. Narayana Guru, *op. cit.*, *Jāti Mīmāṁsā*.

9. Kind, thought of carefully, is but a mould devised by the caster called consciousness. Whatever is cast in it and appears to be, undergoes the same process of being recast and reappearing variously for ever.

10. It is known as 'kind' just because it enables us to discern what something is. No knowing of anything specific happens without the sense of 'kind'.[2]

Why Can't it be Advantageously Used?

Why can't casteism be treated as a social actuality that could be put to better use by encouraging a sort of healthy competition amongst different groups of adepts in certain trades? This question was put to the Guru by his disciple — later his wisdom successor — Nataraja Guru, as he was just out of university with a Master's Degree. The immediate reaction from the Guru was thus: how can something unreal and baseless be a firm basis for any healthy competition in society? It is to be admitted first that casteism is a phantasm perceived only because of ignorance.

Social Movements

Eager as he was to root out casteism, the Guru thought of having a popular organisation of mere humans to fight casteism and its ills. Such an organisation did actually come into existence, but eventually it ended up in becoming an organised force of the particular caste group in which the Guru himself was supposedly born. The irony is that this organisation became the inspiring force for other caste-groups to organise themselves to fight for their own interests. The end result is that no caste group is there, at least in the State of Kerala in India, that has not become an organised force. The Guru finally felt constrained to openly disown the very body which he took pains to rear and to which he gave all his blessings, and of which he was supposed to be the life-long president. What all this indicates is this: even those who were very close to the Guru did not have the insight to understand the Guru and his philosophy and ideals fully.

---

2. Narayana Guru, *op. cit., Jāti Lakṣaṇam,* Verses 8, 9, and 10.

It, in fact, is not surprising. The profuse words of praise showered on the Guru even by great people like Rabindranath Tagore, were for wrong reasons. The poet, for example, when he visited the Guru at his *āśrama* in Varkala, commended the great things the Guru was doing. The Guru reacted immediately, "We have no power of our own to do anything". This came as a surprise to those who were around. Even when in the midst of a widespread social re-awakening that was mounting up, even when he was giving all moral support to it, the Guru could well remain a recluse, an *akartā*, one who has no *karma* of one's own. He always remained fully liberated from all social commitments and obligations. Such was his state of being a *mukta*, the liberated one.

18

Religion

> A set of beliefs concerning the cause, nature and purpose of the universe, especially when considered as the creation of a superhuman agency or agencies, usually involving devotional and ritual observances, and often containing moral codes governing the conduct of human affairs.

THIS is how the *Random House Dictionary* defines 'Religion'. According to this definition, it involves three factors:

1. A set of beliefs as to the origin, nature and purpose of the world.
2. Devotional and ritual observances.
3. A moral code to govern human conduct.

The first is what the entire philosophy we examined in Part I of this study tried to clarify in the Guru's own way, with the difference that no belief in any dogma is insisted upon. Instead, we are guided by the Guru to search freely and scientifically, to arrive at certainty on our own. The credibility of this certainty attains consummation in its experiential realisation. The second aspect is to be dealt with in detail in the next chapter. And the Guru's stand on the third point was our topic of Chapter 15.

None of these three points, themselves, pose a problem in the modern age. What causes the torment is the persisting rivalry and feud among various religious followings. In the wake of this pressing need have come up movements suggesting, "Why can't we do away with religions all together?" Here arises the problem, "What is the role of religion in human life?"

The Role of Religion

Human existence is a part of the existence of the whole, over which man has no control. Yet, by nature, man is a being endowed with a free will. He uses it to chalk out his life with a view to actualising the goal of life he freely conceives. In fact, it is this sense of freedom to choose one's goal of life as well as the way of attaining it that makes life meaningful for man.

But this sense of freedom is curtailed by one exigency: one has no control over what happens, even to oneself, as part of the flow of the total nature. Regardless of whether one is considered to be good or bad, one can only abide by what naturally happens. This point is made clear by Narayana Guru in the *Ātmopadeśa Śatakam* at the beginning of the section that deals with religion. He says:

> Even those who perform meritorious deeds (*sukr̥tis*) are helplessly caught in the whirling action of *prakr̥ti* and thus do revolve.[1]

One of the most basic of all human urges is to be saved from the contingency of untoward and unexpected specific events (*vikr̥tis*) of *prakr̥ti*. The more one makes deliberate efforts towards this end, the more they become fruitless. Here comes the necessity in human life of harmonising the free will of a person with the will of nature, otherwise known as 'destiny'.

Effecting this harmonisation alone can make human life peaceful, and two ways alone are open to make it possible: one is bending the will of nature to abide by the will of humans, and two is to upgrade the human free will and desire so as to be in tune with the will of nature. The former, as everyone knows, is impossible, for despite all the advancement of science, humans are quite unfamiliar with the way *prakr̥ti* unfolds its events. How can something unknown

1. Narayana Guru, *op. cit.*, *Ātmopadeśa Śatakam*, Verse 43.

be brought under one's control? The method of harmonisation alone, then, is practical. It, in effect, means a person surrendering one's will and desires to the unknowable will and desires of *prakṛti* with a willingness to make one's life flow as one with the flow of nature. All these ideas are suggested by the Guru in Verse 43 of the *Ātmopadeśa Śatakam*, of which a part was quoted above.

This harmonisation, in fact, is what religion enables man to attain. Even atheists who avowedly denounce all religions, have their own religion, for they too suggest an alternative way for man to harmonize himself with the total.

Religions postulate a third factor that controls or underlies both the individual and the total. For prophetic religions such as Judaism, Christianity and Islam, this third factor is a personal God who created everything, who controls everything. The individual's duty is simply leading a life following the way commanded by God. Such commandments come to humanity through prophets, the messengers of God, and strictly adhering to them makes one happy in this life. A happy hereafter is also promised. These religions differ only with regard to matters such as who the acceptable prophet is, certain details such as the importance given to values like love and brotherhood, and specific injunctions concerning day-to-day affairs, whereas the core teaching of all of them remains the same. Such differences on which they differ are attributable more to the spatial and temporal exigencies of the origin of those religions than to what the religions basically teach.

A religion by necessity originates from some particular cultural, historical and geographical background. References to injunctions, meaningful only when related to such background aspects, are unavoidable in the words of all prophets, and therefore in the body of the scriptures as well. Practical matters have naturally to vary from place to place, from time to time. Such details kept apart, all prophetic religions fully agree as regards their basic teachings: one, believing in one God alone as the creator and sustainer of all the worlds, and two, the importance of man's willingness to obey His commands. God, being one, cannot give essentially different teachings to humans.

The non-prophetic religions like Hinduism, Buddhism and Jainism, instead of postulating a God high in heaven, perceive one Reality as underlying all that appears to be here. Either called *Brahman* or *dharma*, this Reality unfolds itself, or rolls on beginningless and endless, resulting in the world and its inhabitants appearing to be real. Revisualising this one Reality in all of us culminates in identifying ourselves with It. Our problems also vanish in It.

Whether through believing in one God and obeying His commandments, or through realising one's inseparable oneness with the absolute Reality, what one ultimately gains is relating properly the being of oneself with the being of the Total. This, in effect, is one identifying one's personal will and desires with those of the total being. This being a goal to be attained by every person individually, religion is a personal matter. Attributing social dimensions to it mixes things up and creates the problems we face today.

This attainment of the awareness of oneness, in experience, becomes a contentment in life; not just a pleasing one, but one that makes one capable of treating both pleasure and pain with a sense of equanimity, as a natural part of life. This is attained not by any deliberate action (*karma*) but by effortlessly subjugating oneself to God's will or desirelessly allowing oneself to flow with the total flow of nature. The *karma*s one performs in this state of full identity with the total, in effect, become *akarma*s (non-actions) for the reason that, not the individual but the total is the doer of those *karma*s.

Religion in the Age of Science

Once this core-secret of all religions become known to religionists, all rivalries and feuds among them disappear. In other words, all such antagonisms are the result of a blind-foldedness which prevents one from seeing the essential teaching of the very religion one follows. What we desperately need in this Age of Science, in which the entire world has already turned out to be a global village, is the reawakening of believers of all religions to the heart of what their own religion teaches. Religion then may become something that enhances human dignity based on a scientificity of its own.

This certitude made the Guru declare openly: many religions, in their content, are essentially one. Those who argue for or against any particular religion are compared to the well-known story of a few blind men seeing an elephant — the one who feels the elephant's leg claims, the elephant looks like a pillar; the other who feels its tail says, it is broom-like; the third feeling its ears, asserts an elephant is like a winnowing fan in shape. None of them is wrong, but none of them is right either. What each acquires is simply a partial knowledge and this always allows room for disputations. So it is with the defenders of religions as well. One religion becomes respectable and another despicable only because of the partial understanding about religion each one has. To quote the Guru's own words:

> The ignoramus, unaware of the oneness of the essential core of all religions, like the blind men on seeing an elephant, do meander in distress, with many logical arguments of their own. One has to remain firm, unaffected by such.[2]

It is not possible to defeat any religion through fighting, for every religion has for its strength at its core the high value factor that makes of it a religion. One religion attacking another, for this very reason, results not in the destruction of the targeted religion, but only of the persons who fight. The discriminating, therefore, always keep themselves away from such fights.

A Christian hopes the world one day will follow Christianity; a Muslim expects to convert the entire world to Islam; a Buddhist feels happy if the entire human race embraces Buddhism; a Hindu, though religious conversion does not form part of the creed of Hinduism, always would be happy if the entire world adopts its way of life. But none of them realises the fact that all these mutually exclusive hopes will never be materialised, for the zeal of every religionist is equally strong and equally meaningful.

---

2. Narayana Guru, *op. cit., Ātmopadeśa Śatakam,* Verse 44.

The Psychology of Religious Identity

Why do people become willing even to sacrifice themselves for the cause of the religion they believe in?

Unmindful or ignorant of the many ways availabe to approach the one final goal of identifying oneself with the whole, they think the one way they are familiar with alone is at one's disposal, and that all the others simply misguide people. In the place of the total Reality with which they are intended to be identified, they wrongly find identity with a particular way of approach to it, with a particular religion. An individual, in the state of identity with the whole, becomes nothing, as a drop becomes nothing when fallen into the ocean. The same happens to those who find themselves one with a particular religion also — they feel lost in the being of religion. In the ideal identity with the whole that all religions aim at, the individual feels the blissfulness of realising God or realising the Absolute. On the other hand, the identity with a particular religion creates the impression that the individual sacrificing himself physically is blissful or is doing service to God. The noblest of all gains that all religions promise, thus ends up in becoming the most ignoble of all losses. In either case, there is the common factor of one forgetting one's identity with being an individual entity and finding a new identity with something very abstract, ideal and of high value.

Transmuting one's identity with closed religions into an open one with God or the Absolute is the best solution to the prevailing problem of religious rivalry. The pity is that only the wise, very few in number, realise this. Most of the believers remain ignorant of this. Instead of making life blissful through religiousness, they find blissfulness in sacrificing the very life meant to be made blissful. Only a little of discrimination and wisdom, and going one step further, are required to make one shift the identity from a particular religion to the one goal of all religions. It also results in the living experience of non-dual blissfulness. All these are suggestively summarised by the Guru in Verse 48 of his *Ātmopadeśa Śatakam* as follows:

> The embodied Reality having become confined to a body in its capacity as the bodiless abstract substance, feels the sense of identity such as 'This is mine', or 'That is mine'. The secret of this having become known, one readily attains experiential enlightenment.[3]

Then alone dawns the essential oneness of all religions, or the one Religion or Faith the Guru visualises. Clarifying this point, the Guru says:

> Everyone always makes all kinds of efforts aimed at attaining Self-happiness alone. In this regard, all are of one Faith in this world. With this awareness attained, one should subdue one's own mind so as to keep oneself away from all ungodlinesses.[4]

Matam is the original word the Guru used for religion. This word means also 'opinion', 'well thought-out conclusion', 'a thought', 'idea', 'belief' or 'view'. The oneness of *matam* conceived by the Guru thus has significance much wider in scope than what ardent religionists might conceive. The Guru's well-known dictum, 'whichever the *matam*, it suffices if it betters man' is to be understood in this light.

God-Realisation

God-realisation, the one goal all religions conceive of, in experiential terms, is portrayed by the Guru thus:

> The ever-appearing and ever-disappearing experiences emerge first, and then they sway back and forth assuming the forms both of mind and matter. And thus the Real becomes darkened (as apparent forms) in a thousand ways, and then all of them roll back to their restful abode, finally to merge in its own splendour. Even philosophically perceiving thus is not wisdom. One should, instead, become

3. Narayana Guru, *op. cit., Ātmopadeśa Śatakam,* Verse 48.
4. *Op. cit.,* Verse 49.

> a bee that gently falls into the honey-filled core of the lotus (God) and with its gentle murmer be there for ever in the ecstacy of blissfulness![5]

Into this non-dual experience become merged all philosophical understanding concerning the cause and nature of the world, all devotional and ritual observances, and all moral codes of human conduct. In it terminates all religiousness.

The Parliament of Religions

It is this realisation of the essential oneness of all religions that inspired Narayana Guru to organise a Parliament of Religions in Aluva at his own initiative in 1924. This was the first ever such get-together of religious leaders in Asia. At the entrance to the venue were written as specifically directed by the Guru, the words: 'Meant not for arguing and winning, but for knowing and letting know'. At the conclusion of this Parliament the Guru decided to start an advanced study centre for religions at his own headquarters *āśrama* at Śivagiri. The materialisation of this wish actually took place as the East-West University of Brahmavidya, which is a part of the Narayana Gurukula Movement.

---

5. Narayana Guru, *op. cit., Jananī-Navarathna-Mañjarī*: Verse 3.

19

God, Temples, Rites

Narayana Guru, an enlightened person, was honoured by everyone, irrespective of their walk of life or view of life. His vision being all-comprehensive and unitive, no one could see an outlander in him, and more, those of different perceptions had the feeling that the Guru was with them. Even atheists were there among his close followers.

Was he a believer? Yes; only that it is rather in a scientific sense. God, the one Reality that underlies everything that appears to be in all the worlds, here or the hereafter, was more than a matter of belief for the Guru. Admitting the existence of the world means admitting the realness of God, for the world cannot appear to be without a causal Reality underlying. Likewise, admitting God means admitting the existence of the world as the apparent form in which God becomes manifest. God, *ātman*, *Brahman*, *aṟivu* (*cit*) were interchangeable terms to him. God and the world are inseparably one, as are water and waves, as are gold and ornaments.

Does God exist? The direct answer to this question derivable from the Guru's philosophy would be, "God alone exists; all that appear as forming the world are simply various manifestations of the one God". Can you see God then? Yes, God alone is what you see always; you simply mistake it as the world.

Why Prayer

The ultimate goal a seeker or supplicant can attain is finding oneself one with God, *Brahman*, *ātman*, or *aṟivu*. If this non-duality is what the Guru teaches, what then is the need for any prayer at all? Prayer is relevant only when the supplicant thinks of oneself as separate from God. At the same time, almost all the hymns written by the Guru have in them an element of prayer. The universal prayer, *Daiva-Daśakam*, is purely a prayer all through, though replete with his philosophical vision of non-duality. God, in that work, is defined as *satyam-jñānam-ānandam*, equivalent to the Upaniṣadic dictum *sat-cit-ānandam*. This prayer, as is the case of his numerous hymns, is in the form of a supplication made by the ignorant for the attainment of the wisdom of non-duality. The beginning of this prayer, for example, is in the form of an entreaty for the protective caring of God conceived of as existing high in heaven, more reminiscent of the perception of prophetic religions. But the tone makes an about-turn as the work concludes. The prayer then is that of a Vedāntic seeker for his final merger in the ocean of the splendour of God, and for experiencing the eternal Happiness of being eternally one with God. In the Guru's own words:

> Into the deep ocean of Your splendour, let all of us become merged, to live in it eternally in the plenitude of Happiness.[1]

In another hymn on Śiva, the Guru goes to the extent of saying:

> O God, please keep in mind that I do not have any desire other than attaining straightaway the state in which you and I become one.[2]

God, One or Many?

Narayana Guru admits the existence of one God only, or rather of one God alone as having real existence. Why did he then install various deities in temples and compose hymns in praise of them? Gaṇapati, Viṣṇu, Śiva, Devī, Subrahmaṇya are such deities. His praising many deities does not mean he admits of more than one God. The oneness of God and multiplicity of deities are not to be confused. A particular deity Guru praises is neither seen by him, nor meant to be seen by others, as one among many gods, but only as

1. Narayana Guru, *op. cit.*, *Daiva-Daśakam*, Verse 10.
2. *Op. cit.*, *Sadāśiva Darśanam*, Verse 5.

symbolising the one ultimate Reality in a particular way. For example, refer to the *Jananī-Navaratna-Mañjarī* verse quoted in the last chapter and the *Tevāra-Patikam* verse quoted earlier in Chapter 14. One God seen from different angles of value-perception on different occasions, appears to assume a different image in the mind of a poet-genius, each such image forming a different deity. The more a deity is pondered upon, the more the mystery of the one God becomes clear. In fact, such images installed in temples are known as *vigrahas*, meaning, 'something to be pondered upon in a specific way'. The poet in the Guru sees the many deities as representing the one *Brahman*. The *ṛṣi* in him sees the one *Brahman* in which become merged all the different deities. Deities are merely poetically-sublime linguistic devices that he skillfully utilises to give expression to the one *Brahman* in experiential terms.

Once, it became a point of contention between two groups of the local people as to which should be the deity to be installed in the newly built temple. The Guru resolved the dispute by suggesting a third novel one. In the place of a deity, the Guru installed a large mirror with its silver coating behind partly scraped out in the shape of the Malayālam letter for *AUṀ ŚĀNTIḤ*. The mirror reflects oneself. God is also to be perceived as reflected in oneself. God and Self are both symbolised by *AUṀ*.

Temples

It is well known that in philosophy Narayana Guru followed the line of thought of Śaṅkara. Again like Śaṅkara, owing to historical exigencies, the Guru also had to install deities — either of Śiva, Devī or Subrahmaṇya — in many temples. The first one was the Śiva Temple at Aruvipuram near Neyyattinkara, Kerala. The installation of this temple was an epoch-making event, for it was for the first time that a person outside the orthodox priestly fold dared to officiate the installing of a deity. This new move gave impetus to an unprecedented demand at various places for more such temples, open to all with no caste discrimination. The existing orthodox temples were not open to those of the lower strata, though their offerings either in kind or cash were readily accepted. A chunk of such offerings, with the advent of the new type of temples, began to flow towards them. This should also be counted as one of the forces that compelled the state authorities to concede to formally let open all temples to all Hindus, through the much acclaimed 'Temple Entry Proclamation of the Maharaja of Travancore'.

Temples, in the perception of the Guru, are not merely places of worship. They have as well to serve as the focal point for the cultural advancement of the concerned localities. Each temple was to have an open area for people to get together formally and informally to discuss matters of higher value. This was to be supported by the addition of a library attached to the temple.

The deity installed in a temple is not just meant for worshipping and asking for favours. The hymns the Guru composed at the time of installing deities clarify what he intended the people to understand, with the deity as a means. Every deity, in his perception, is a visual means that helps the supplicant attain the non-dual experience, provided, of course, the supplicant is a seeker as well. In short, a new perception of over-all education was there in the mind of the Guru when he conceived the idea of the new type of temples.

Nearly eighty such temples came up, but none of them, or rather none of their promoters, did rise to the level of perception the Guru dreamed of. He, therefore, at a later stage, discouraged people from establishing more new temples; instead, he asked them to build new schools so that education in a more direct and formal way could be made available to the public. Only after reaching a certain stage of formal education will the informal education the Guru thought of normally work. He took initiative himself to start an English School at Śivagiri, Varkala and a Sanskrit School at Aluva.

Rites

Of course all the newly started temples were to practise ritualistic worship in the traditional way. Many interested youth of the non-priestly section of the society began to get trained as temple-priests. Nevertheless, the Guru never was a ritualist. He always remained a *jñānin*, a wisdom teacher *par excellence*. As such, he was well aware of the meaninglessness of rituals in a wisdom context, as is stated directly by him in the second verse of his *Jananī-Navaratna-Mañjarī*, thus:

> All that emerges and looms owing to the non-existent *māyā*, has no being other than that of pure and unconditioned consciousness (*aṟivu*);
>
> Air, rocks (earth), ocean (water), fire and the space empty — all these are nothing but one primordial Consciousness self-unfolded;
>
> Their easily-known-insignificance, when realised and taught, makes valueless all the Vedic rituals. The searching mind becomes bewildered no more;
>
> The gaining of this one existent reality (*sat*), the One everyone is in search of, alone is what I pray for. O the easily-accessible, self-emanating Consciousness-mother![3]

Yet, he was not totally against rituals. No human society exists that does not practise ritualism in one way or another. How was ritualism originated? Thinking is considered to be the characteristic that differentiates humans from other animals. To think means to conceive ideas. Giving expression to such ideas also forms part of human nature, and such expressions can adopt anything as their medium. In some cases, ideas find expression in the form of certain actions. The meaning of such actions is more than their immediate outcome. They communicate something to others and to posterity, of a higher meaning and a long-standing value. In every human civilisation in the world, such symbolic actions prevail. Such actions of symbolic significance are what we call rites. Even politics and statecraft, often quite unrelated to religion, abound with such rituals. The original message of such actions relating to the ultimate meaning of life, later became abstruse, and the action alone became all that mattered in the hands of priestcraft.

---

3. Narayana Guru, *op. cit.*, *Jananī-Navaratna-Mañjarī*: Verse 2.

Every ritualistic action thus has something sublime to convey to us. Rediscovering this wisdom significance of rituals later became a necessity, especially by the time of the advent of the Upaniṣads. The entire text of the *Chāndogya Upaniṣad*, we should note, is an attempt in an elabarate way to recover the forgotten wisdom significance of the simple rite of *udgītha*-chanting that forms part of the elaborate ritual known as *Soma Yāga*. The Upaniṣad, by accomplishing this, unfolds the entire spectrum of the highest wisdom known as *brahma-vidyā* or *ātma-vidyā*. Narayana Guru also had the same attitude towards rituals. Almost all his hymns are suggestive of this attitude and it is directly perceptible in the revisualised fire-sacrifice he suggested for which he composed a new *mantra*. It reads thus:

> *AUṀ agne tava yat tejas tad brāhmam*
> *atas tvam pratyakṣam brahmāsi*
> *tvadiyā indriyāṇi mano-buddhir iti sapta-jihvāḥ*
> *tvayi viṣayā iti samidho juhomi*
> *aham ity ājyam juhomi*
> *tvam naḥ prasīda prasīda*
> *śreyaśca preyaśca prayaccha svāha.*[4]

> O fire, this brightness of yours pertains to *Brahman*. For this reason, I consider you as *Brahman* become perceptible. Your seven tongues (*sapta-jihvāḥ*) are the five sense-organs, mind and intellect. Unto you I offer all the corresponding objects as oblation. Then I offer myself in the form of clarified butter. Be pleased with us, be pleased with us! And please grant us the favour of attaining the highest goal of life as well as having worldly gains. *Svāhā*!

This *mantra* that sounds like a Vedic one, shows how an ordinary fire sacrifice could be made sublime as a demonstrative lesson of higher wisdom. The burning fire, effulgence in essence, stands for *Brahman*. Into it are offered as oblation all that is objectively perceptible, i.e., the entire world, and finally the sacrificer or the subject as well. What remains then is *Brahman* alone. All the pleasures and pains of life are then felt simply as the sacred remnants (*prasād*)

4. Narayana Guru, *op. cit., Homa Mantra*.

of the fire-sacrifice. This enlightenment bestows on us the highest happiness of wisdom along with all the worldly needs provided for. In this one *mantra* is thus condensed by the Guru, the entire teaching of the *Chāndogya Upaniṣad*, an extensive text that runs to eight long chapters.

Such is the subtle way in which the Guru admitted ritualism into the precincts of wisdom. Śaṅkara thought, mixing up of ritualism with wisdom was an error which he called *jñāna-karma-samuccaya*. Narayana Guru, on the other hand, shows how *karma* could be made use of as a means for imparting wisdom, thus effecting the yogic harmony of *karma* and *jñāna*, a way that could well be called *jñāna-karma-samanvaya*. In fact, his life itself was a demonstration of *jñāna-karma-samanvaya*.

Appendix

The Works of Narayana Guru

Philosophical Works

1. *ĀTMOPADEŚA ŚATAKAM: ONE HUNDRED VERSES OF SELF-INSTRUCTION* (in Malayālam)

This is the text in which the Guru expounds his philosophy in its entirety, stating that there exists only one Reality — the *ātman*, unconditioned Consciousness in essence. This is the entity that pervades through all beings, from the mind, the subtlest of manifestations, to the limitless physical world, the grossest of manifestations, like waves emerging and remerging in ocean. Just as these waves cannot exist separately from the ocean, the world and everything in it, including oneself, cannot exist apart from *ātman*, which is also known as *Brahman*. Inherent within *ātman* is the mysterious *māyā*, the power that causes all illusory phenomena to appear within itself. The world thus takes form, branching into the internal subjective world and the external objective world. In essence, ultimately everything becomes reduced to *sat-cit-ānanda*. The Guru considers one's transitory existence as a wave formed in the ocean of *sat-cit-ānanda* and, therefore, one is that *sat-cit-ānanda*.

A sage of the Age of Science, Narayana Guru restates *brahma-vidyā* from a scientific point of view, yet the word *Brahman* does not appear in this work at all. Instead, the emphasis is given to *ātmā* or *aham*, unconditioned Consciousness (*aṟivu*) in essence, which perception helps to resolve many of the philosophical riddles more easily.

2. *DARŚANA-MĀLĀ: GARLAND OF VISIONS* (in Sanskrit)

In this work, the Guru concisely presents Vedānta as the Science of sciences and makes clear once more the essence of the Upaniṣadic wisdom. Written in the traditional scholastic style, this work visualises the one ultimate Reality, *Brahman* or *ātman*, from different philosophical perspectives. *Darśana-Mālā* is written in ten chapters with each containing ten verses. The ten chapters consist of the following headings:

(i)	*Adhyāropa-Darśanaṁ*	-	assuming that the world is real.
(ii)	*Apavāda-Darśanam*	-	revoking the assumed world.
(iii)	*Asatya-Darśanam*	-	viewing the world as an imagination of the mind.
(iv)	*Māyā-Darśanam*	-	treating the world as an illusion.
(v)	*Bhāna-Darśanam*	-	treating the world as an aggregate of conditionings that take place in the unconditioned Consciousness.
(vi)	*Karma-Darśanam*	-	looking at one's own life as well as that of the world from the point of view of activities that really take place in the one causal Reality rather than being perfomed by any individual.
(vii)	'*Jñāna-Darśanam*	-	examining one's own knowledge of everything.
(viii)	*Bhakti-Darśanam*	-	relating oneself to the most valuable Reality, *Brahman* or *ātman*, with conviction.
(ix)	*Yoga-Darśanam*	-	the actual practice of attaining the oneness which could be through either *karma-yoga* or *jñāna-yoga*.

(x) *Nirvāṇa-Darśanam* - describing the various levels of experiencing the oneness and Final Absorption.

3. *ADVAITA DĪPIKĀ: THE LAMP OF NON-DUALITY* (in Malayālam)

The essentials of Advaita Vedānta are summarised into nineteen verses by Narayana Guru in this work. The specific question the Guru answers in this work is, "Why the world continues to appear as real to perception, even after becoming convinced of its unreality?"

4. *AṞIVU: CONSCIOUSNESS* (in Malayālam)

This particular work was written in fifteen verses in which Vedānta is restated from an epistemological perspective. Consciousness (*aṟivu*) alone is real. In its absence, the existence or otherwise of anything is irrelevant. *Aṟivu* unravels itself as everything, and is categorised into subjective and objective knowledges, both having eight constituent factors each. Therefore, the subjective and objective aspects of knowledge have a perfect parity. However, these analyses and classifications are meaningful only when we subject the really indivisible *aṟivu* to such imaginary divisions. For even with such analyses and divisions, in reality, *aṟivu* remains indivisible and as one.

5. *DAIVA DAŚAKAM: TEN VERSES ON GOD* (in Malayālam)

A universal prayer that transcends the bounds of all religions. The Guru created this in a simple style, summarising in plain and simple language, the essentials of his philosophical vision. This was written as a common prayer with the intention that it should be recited daily by the children of the *aśrama* he founded at Varkala.

6. *BRAHMAVIDYĀ PAÑCAKAM: BRAHMAVIDYĀ IN FIVE VERSES* (in Sanskrit)

Narayana Guru epitomises Vedānta in five verses in this particular text. The first verse depicts who a real seeker or disciple is; who a real *guru* is; how a mutual rapport is established between the two before the teaching of wisdom takes place; and what questions are asked by the seeker.

The imaginary *guru*, in the second verse, replies: "You are *Brahman* indeed; the world is originated from you."

The third verse describes how *Brahman* is *sat*, the one Substance in all that seems to be.

In the fourh verse the Guru reveals how *Brahman* is *cit* (Consciousness).

The final verse explains how *Brahman* is experienced in actual life as the blissful state (*ānanda*) of non-duality, free from all bondages caused by the illusions of *karma*.

7. *VEDĀNTA SŪTRAS* (in Sanskrit)

The essentials of Vedānta are condensed into twenty four *sūtra*s. This is the first ever *sūtra* text written on Vedānta since the *Bādarāyaṇa-Sūtras* created more than two thousand years ago.

8. *NIRVṚTI PAÑCAKAM: FIVE VERSES ON FINAL ABSORPTION* (in Sanskrit)

Narayana Guru wrote these verses when he visited Ramaṇa Maharṣi at Thiruvaṇṇāmalai. It portrays the external signs visible in those who are fully absorbed in *Brahman*.

9. *ŚLOKA TRAYĪ: THREE VERSES* (in Sanskrit)

These three verses are on how and why the one underlying Substance (*dharmī*) is neither perceptible nor inferable. What we perceive or infer about are its attributes (*dharma*s) only.

10. *HOMA MANTRA: A MANTRA FOR BURNT SACRIFICE* (in Sanskrit)

This *mantra* has resemblance of Vedic *mantra*s and it is meant to be chanted while performing a new type of burnt sacrifice. The fire into which offerings are made in this burnt sacrifice is *Brahman*. The offerings are the aggregate of objects of the senses, the mind and the intellect. 'I' or the one who makes these oblations is also finally offered into the fire of *Brahman*. It is a ritual of pure wisdom import.

Hymns

1. *VINĀYAKA AṢṬAKAM: EIGHT VERSES ON VINĀYAKA OR GAṆAPATI* (in Sanskrit)

In this song of praise, the Guru visualises Vināyaka, symbolically representing the Absolute, as the one adored by both gods and men.

2. *ŚRĪ VĀSUDEVA AṢṬAKAM: EIGHT VERSES ON VĀSUDEVA OR VIṢṆU* (in Sanskrit)

Viṣṇu is seen as a *yogī* with a well-balanced state of existence, while at the same time, he is attributed with all the mythologically accepted qualities.

3. *VIṢṆU AṢṬAKAM: EIGHT VERSES ON VIṢṆU* (in Sanskrit)

Here, Viṣṇu is adored in his traditionally worshipped form. The supplicant thinks of himself as a humble servant to Viṣṇu, a concept very dear to the Vaiṣṇavites.

4. *ŚRĪKṚṢṆA DARŚANAM: A VISION OF ŚRĪ KṚṢṆA* (in Malayālam)

While the Guru was still a student at Vāraṇappally he had a vision of Kṛṣṇa. This work is an extemporaneous exposition of that ecstatic vision.

5. *ŚIVAPRASĀDA PAÑCAKAM: FIVE VERSES ON THE GRACE OF ŚIVA* (in *Malayālam*)

The Guru praises Śiva's graceful willingness to safeguard those who suffer from the infatuations of lust and other aspects of the material world.

6. *SADĀŚIVA DARŚANAM: A VISION OF THE ETERNAL ŚIVA* (in Malayālam)

Written in a rhythmic and alliterative diction, this work praises Śiva as the cause of the phenomenal world, as well as our saviour from all its miseries. This redemption gives us the opportunity to dance as one with him, ecstatically and eternally.

7. *ŚIVA SATAKAM: ONE HUNDRED VERSES ON ŚIVA* (in Malayālam)

It is assumed that this was written when the Śiva Temple at Aruvippuṟam was consecrated. These verses are a revelatory head-to-foot description of the symbolic figure of Śiva, followed by a series of upsurging visions based on various characteristics of the Śiva concept, each brimming with a sublime mystical ecstacy, clothed in equally sublime poetical imageries. A high degree of intimacy is constantly maintained between the Guru and the deity, and with the desire to lead a celibate's life, he prays to Śiva, the destroyer of Kāma (Eros), to save him from the temptations of lust. What he seeks to attain finally are the holy feet of Śiva — the only refuge from carnal temptations — and the eternal joy of *Śiva sāyujya* (the blissfulness of being one with Śiva).

8. *ARDHANĀRĪŚVARA STAVAM: A HYMN TO THE ANDROGYNOUS ŚIVA* (in Malayālam)

This was written when southern India was severely gripped by the effects of an unprecedented drought. The Guru takes the liberty to humorously rebuke Śiva for letting the people suffer for want of water whilst he carries all the water in his matted hair. Unbelievably enough, it rained heavily immediately upon the recital of this hymn.

9. *MANANĀTĪTAM: BEYOND COMPREHENSION* (in Malayālam)

A hymn of ten verses praising Śiva mainly as the destroyer of Kāma (Eros). The Guru explains that taking refuge in Śiva is the only way to save oneself from the clutches of carnal temptations and to finally achieve the eternal happiness of *Śiva sāyujya*.

10. *CIJJAḌA CINTANAM: REFLECTIONS ON MIND AND MATTER* (in Malayālam)

The Guru makes clear in this particular work that what we differentiate as mind and matter are but two apparent manifestations of the one Absolute Reality, represented here by Śiva. With this realisation, the concept of the mind-matter duality vanishes.

11. *KUṆḌALINĪ PĀṬṬU: SONG OF KUṆḌALINĪ SNAKE* (in Malayālam)

A song praising Śiva and addressed to one's own mind conceived as a dancing snake.

12. *INDRIYA VAIRĀGYAM: DETACHMENT FROM THE PLEASURES OF THE SENSES* (in Malayālam)

Again referring to Śiva, this composition of ten verses describes how one can finally visualise Śiva both outside and inside, by internalising one's own perceptions. This is because the senses, along with their external objects, are habitually outward-facing and are therefore a hinderance in perceiving Śiva as the one underlying Reality in all of them.

13. *PRAPAÑCA SṚṢṬI: THE CREATION OF THE WORLD* (in Malayālam)

Once again praising Śiva in ten verses, this work depicts how the illusory appearance of this objective world and the subjective aspect that perceives it, all have their source in the one body of Śiva. The supplicant's final entreaty to Śiva is for his own worldly body to be absorbed into that of Śiva.

14. *KOLATĪREŚA STAVAM: HYMN TO KOLATĪREŚA* (in Malayālam)

Praising the deity of Śiva installed by the Guru at the Kolathukara (Kolatīra) in Kulathur near Trivandrum. This is a highly melodious and rhythmic hymn in which the Guru prays to Śiva to bless him with an ideally happy life, within the vicinity of His abode, free from all sufferings. Yet he concludes by admitting that all these prayers are simply childish and meaningless.

15. *SVĀNUBHAVA GĪTI: THE LYRIC REVELATION OF THE REALISED SELF* (in Malayālam)

This is the song of one hundred verses in the *antādi* style (a literary style in which the last word of every verse and the first word of the succeeding verse are the same). A free flowing song in which spiritual discipline, philosophical enquiry, attainment of certitude and mystical vision, and finally its ecstacy, are predominant, while yet again the figure of Śiva surfaces frequently. Forty verses of this unique work have yet to be restored.

16. *PIṆḌA NANDĪ: FOETAL GRATITUDE* (in Malayālam)

The Guru praises Śiva as the one who protects the embryo while it remains helpless in the darkness of the mother's womb. This is a unique but realistic concept of the protective role of God.

17. *CITAMBARA AṢṬAKAM: EIGHT VERSES ON MENTAL SPACE* (in Sanskrit)

In praise of the *Śivaliṅga* (the phallic symbol representing Śiva and signifying the creative vitality of the Absolute, always resting in the *yoni* which symbolising the female equivalent). The Reality represented by the *liṅga* is praised equally by all gods and men, thus trascends the limits of all the worlds. At the same time, it is perceived in the boundless space of one's own mind.

18. *TEVĀRA PATIKANKAL* (in Tamil)

Five songs praising Śiva, resembling those of the great Śaiva saints such as Nalvar.

19. *A SINGLE TAMIL VERSE PRAISING ŚIVA*

This is a single verse in Tamil praising Lord Śiva.

20. *DEVĪ STAVAM: A HYMN TO DEVĪ* (in Malayālam)

The Mother-Goddess is visualised as the embodiment of the Final Silence — the culmination of all wisdom teaching. The supplicant prays to Devī to breathe into him the secret of Silence of which she is the essence. It is explained in this piece of work that all beings, including the Guru, are mirage-like and deceptive. The only way to achieve any satisfaction in life is to become aware of the need to be one with Devī.

21. *MAṆṆANTALA DEVĪ STAVAM: HYMN TO THE DEVĪ AT MAṆṆANTALA* (in Malayālam)

This is a unique piece consisting of nine verses, each in a different metre. The Guru wrote this when he installed the deity of Devī at Maṇṇantala, a place near Trivandrum. There is nothing that is impossible to Devī, and when one realises that such a Devī exists within oneself, nothing is felt impossible.

22. *KĀLĪ NĀṬAKAM: THE DANCE-DRAMA OF KĀLĪ* (in Malayālam)

This matchless, non-stop song is in praise of Kālī, the Mother-Goddess. Her cosmic dance of momentarily changing moods presents itself in the form of an ever-changing world and its life. Just as the facial expressions of a dancer varies from one moment to the next, so too does the world. We are so engrossed in our own irregular moods and the pleasures and pains they bring, that we are oblivious to Devī who remains constant and yet generates all these changes.

23. *JANANĪ NAVARATNA MAÑJARĪ: A NINE-GEMMED BOUQUET ON THE MOTHER* (in Malayālam)

This was written when the foundation stone for the Śāradā Temple at Śivagiri, Varkala, was laid by the Guru. It addresses the Mother as the personification of wisdom. Although this is a hymn, its contents elucidate Vedānta in a highly melodious diction using an alliterative style of poetical language throughout. This work concludes with the attainment of the state of wisdom that is beyond words.

24. *BHADRAKĀLĪ AṢṬAKAM: EIGHT VERSES ON BHADRAKĀLĪ* (in Sanskrit)

Describing Bhadrakālī (the most auspicious Goddess with a dark external appearance) in her different moods. The exquisiteness of the language is more prominent than the profoundity of its contents. The first half of almost all the verses consists of one compound word running into as many as 38 syllables which flow freely in a wave-like fashion. This particular work provides conclusive evidence of how greatly the Guru was at ease with the Sanskrit language.

25. *ṢAṆMUKHA STOTRAM: A HYMN TO ṢAṆMUKHA, THE SIX-HEADED GOD* (in Malayālam)

In praise of Subrahmaṇya, this work contains 19 verses, each beginning with, in sequence, a letter of the Malayālam alphabet. The first part of the text describes the physical form of Subrahmaṇya from head to foot, relating each part to a philosophical and mystical implication. The rest of the work revises some of the concepts in Vedānta and Yoga, as would be done by a devout supplicant. This is concluded with a touch of humour.

26. *ṢAṆMUKHA DAŚAKAM: TEN VERSES ON ṢAṆMUKHA* (in Malayālam)

This is a highly poetical and symbolic head-to-foot description of Subrahmaṇya's figure.

27. *ṢĀṆMĀTURA STAVAM: HYMN ON ṢĀṆMĀTURA, THE SIX-MOTHER-GOD* (in Sanskrit)

This consists of nine alliterative verses in a highly complex metre praising Subrahmaṇya in his different moods.

28. *SUBRAHMAṆYA KĪRTAṆAM: IN PRAISE OF SUBRAHMAṆYA* (in Malayālam)

Subrahmaṇya is visualised as having ascended king-like in a highly protected fortress. The supplicant, a begger, attempts to reach him, and he succeeds. On reaching there, he finds his oneness with Subrahmaṇya, a state in which he feels relaxed to the extent that he shows a sense of humour towards Him. The first and the last verses describe Śiva as the father of Subrahmaṇya, and the remaining verses are addressed to Subrahmaṇya directly. A touch of revision given to some notions prevailing in the Vedānta and Yoga systems is apparent in this work.

29. *NAVA MAÑJARĪ: A BOUQUET OF NINE VERSES* (in Malayālam)

Written at the instance of Sri Chaṭṭampi Swāmi, this is a work unparalleled in Malayālam literature. Strung with chosen words of rare usage, unfamiliar even to the *puṇḍit*s of the language, composed in a lengthy and complex meter, it is alliterative throughout. It describes the different moods of Subrahmaṇya, each, in one way or another, providing a source of relief for the humble. Subrahmaṇya is even beseeched upon to save the supplicant from the requirement of any logical evidence for their oneness. Once God's blessings are availed and the oneness attained, of what use is any logical evidence for that oneness?

30. *GUHA AṢṬAKAM: EIGHT VERSES ON GUHA, SUBRAHMAṆYA* (in Sanskrit)

This is a description of the different moods of Subrahmaṇya as seen by the Guru. God, with the entire cosmos for his body, remains within the heart of the supplicant. Each verse ends with the words *praṇamata deveśam guham āveśam* (Adore with all ardour, Guha the chief of gods).

31. *BĀHULEYA AṢṬAKAM: EIGHT VERSES ON BAHULEYA OR SUBRAHMAṆYA* (in Sanskrit)

Written in a sonorous style, this piece sounds like a Tāntric *mantra*. With *OṀ HRĪṀ ŚARAVAṆA BHAVA* for the *bīja mantra* (seed-like chant), the work as a whole looks like a tree that grows out of this seed, each verse sprouting from each of its seed-like syllables *(bīja akṣara*). How Subrahmaṇya could be conceived in the Vedāntic context with all the mythological anecdotes given their due places and depicted in a seemingly Tāntric style, is exemplified by the Guru through this one work.

32. *DEVĪ PRAṆĀMA DEVYĀṢṬAKAM: EIGHT VERSES PAYING OBEISANCE TO DEVĪ* (in Sanskrit)

The Guru describes Devī's changing moods in different contexts, all symbolising various aspects of the one all-supporting creative principle. This was written in a high-sounding alliterative style.

Works of Moral Value

1. *JĪVAKĀRUṆYA PAÑCAKAM: FIVE VERSES ON KINDNESS TO LIFE* (in Malayālam)

The Guru states that we are all manifestations of the one Self. Therefore, in essence, we are all brothers. If one kills another being, that is the same as killing oneself or one's own brother. *Ahiṁsā* (non-hurting) thus becomes natural to those who are aware of this Reality.

2. *ANUKAMPĀ DEŚAKAM: TEN VERSES ON MERCY* (in Malayālam)

Mercy is depicted here as having a high human value and reflects God-consciousness in life. Knowledge makes one merciful, and ignorance creates mercilessness, sowing the seeds of all our miseries. All visionaries and prophets are embodiments of mercy, and as such, they are adored as being equal to God. All the scriptures also teach us this same truth.

3. *JĀTI NIRṆAYAM: THE CRITIQUE OF CASTE*

This is a critical enquiry into the meaninglessness of the caste system. One verse is written in Sanskrit and six are in Malayālam. The famous dictum *'oru jāti, oru matam, oru daivam manuṣyanu'* (One in kind, one in faith, one in God is man) appears in this work. The Guru points out that even Vyāsa, the greatest of all Indian seers, was born as an untouchable outcaste, if at all such a system is to be reckoned with.

4. *JĀTI LAKṢAṆAM: DEFINITION OF JĀTI* (in Malayālam)

The word *jāti* does not really denote caste system. It refers to any particular biological species or kind. If a male and female, through mating, produce offspring, then they belong to one species or *jāti*. The categorising of all things into their genera and species is done in order to distinguish one group from another. It does not have anything to do with the caste system. The Guru states that it is ignorance that makes one ask of another's *jāti*, as it is self-evident from our physical appearance that we all belong to the same kind — the humankind.

5. *SADĀCĀRAM: PATTERN OF GOOD BEHAVIOUR* (in Malayālam)

These are seven verses about morally sound behaviour pattern and its basis.

6. *MUNICARYĀ PAÑCAKAM*: FIVE VERSES ON THE LIFE OF A RECLUSE (in Malayālam)

7. *AHIṀSĀ: NON-HURTING* (in Malayālam)

Five verses extolling the high value of not hurting other living beings, particularly for eating.

8. *ĀŚRAMAM* (in Sanskrit)

The Guru wrote five verses on how to run an *āśrama* when he found that lawyers were unsuccessful at formulating a code of rules for conducting the running of the *āśrama* which he had founded.

9. *DHARMAM* (in Sanskrit)

A verse written greeting a periodical named *Dharmam* published by some of his followers to propagate his teachings.

10. *AN OBITUARY OF TWO VERSES TO SRI CHATTAMPI SWAMI* (in Sanskrit)

11. *COMPLETION OF AN INCOMPLETE VERSE* (in Malayālam)

GREETING TO THE DHARMAKUMARAN MONTHLY (in Malayālam)

12. *SRI NARAYANA SMṚTI* (in Sanskrit)

A compendium of the code of rules of human life written at the Guru's direction, by his disciple Swami Ātmānanda. This is in the form of a dialogue between Sri Narayana Guru and his disciples. As it is considered unbecoming of a *jñānin* to write such a code of rules (*smṛti*), this was done by his disciple. What is always expected of a Guru is the word of wisdom. The *Sri Narayana Smṛti* details the codes of conduct that man needs in his practical life.

Translations

- ***Īśa Upaniṣad***: From the Sanskrit original into Malayālam.
- ***Tirukural***: From the Tamil orginal into Malayālam. From this, only the first four sections have been restored.
- It is belived that the Guru translated the Tamil book *Ozhivil Oḍukkam* into Malayālam. It is yet to be restored.

Prose Works

1. *CIJJAḌA CINTAKAM: REFLECTIONS ON MIND AND MATTER* (in Malayālam)

A detailed prose version of the theme dealt with in the poem *Cijjaḍa Cintanam.*

2. *DAIVA CINTANAM-I: REFLECTIONS ON GOD* (in Malayālam)

An evaluation of the practice of worshipping evil spirits and deities and sacrificing, in order to reveal how barbaric and meaningless they are and to clear the right path of proper worship.

3. *DAIVA CINTANAM-2: REFLECTIONS ON GOD* (in Malayālam)

Expounds the proper concept of God and the proper way of worshipping.

4. *GADYA PRĀRTHANĀ* (in Malayālam)

An ideal prayer in prose form addressed to the Supreme Self.

5. *ĀTMA VILĀSAM: (SELF'S SELF-MANIFESTATION)*

Exposition of an intuitive vision of the glory of God, the Supreme Self, in prose form.

Glossary

Abhayam: Fearlessness. One of the aspects in which the knowledge of *Brahman* is experienced as a value.

Ācārya: A teacher or preceptor. In the Vedāntic context, any of the various commentators on the basic scriptures — the Upaniṣads, *Brahma-Sūtras* of Bādarāyaṇa and the *Bhagavad Gītā*.

Advaita-darśana: Vision of non-duality, the final certitude a seeker aspires after.

Advaita Vedānta: Of the many schools of Vedānta based on different commentaries of different *ācārya*s (see), the one propounded by Śaṅkara.

Āgāmī-karma: (see *karma*).

Agni: Fire; also the presiding deity of fire.

Aham: I; often used by Narayana Guru as a synonym of *ātmā*.

Ahiṁsā: The habit of abstaining from killing or hurting others in thought, word or deed.

Ajāta-vāda: The theory that no creation takes place. Only what exists gets transformed into new forms.

Ajñāna: Ignorance. The mistaken notion concerning oneself and the world that what appears manifestly is real, completely oblivious of the one all-underlying Reality called *Brahman* or *ātman*.

Ākāśa: Space. That which gives room for everything to exist. Also called *vyoman*.

Akhaṇḍa: The indivisible infinite; particularly referring to *ātman* or *Brahman*.

Amṛta: Immorality or the immortal Reality. Poetically imagined as the elixier in a golden pot that emerged from the Milk-Ocean when the *deva*s and *asura*s churned it together.

Amṛtatva: The state of being immortal.

Ānanda (*Ānandam*): Bliss. To be understood in the context of the 'good' in Western philosophy as a supreme value. *Sat, cit* and *ānanda* are terms conjointly used to define the Absolute (*Brahman*) in Vedānta. Concerning an individual being, it is to be understood as the value consciousness that enables one to evaluate one's experiences either as pleasurable or painful.

Ānātmā (*Anātman*): Non-self.

Antarikṣa: Atmosphere. Literally, 'that which is perceived in the middle'. The middle world conceived in the Vedas as existing between the earth and heaven.

Aṇu: Atom. Litterally, 'the indivisible'.

Anya: The other. That kind of knowledge which cognises multiple appearances.

Ap: Water. One of the basic elements of nature.

Aparā: Relativistic, conditional.

Apara-Brahman: Lower *Brahman* as opposed to *para-Brahman* (supreme *Brahman*). The causal Reality conceived as appearing as all the effects.

Aparā-māyā: According to Narayana Guru, the functional aspect of *māyā* (see), because of which the one *Brahman*, Consciousness in essence, manifests itself as objects of sense-perception.

Aṟivu: A Malayālam word for 'knowledge'. Narayana Guru prefers this word, especially when he refers to Pure, Unconditioned Consciousness. The word is also used to denote any kind of knowledge.

Ātmā (*Ātman*): The self (from the root '*āt*', meaning 'to prevade'). The invisible reality or stuff that prevades any visible form. Often confused with *jīva*, the soul. Used in slightly altered senses according to the context. The simplest meaning of the word is 'I' or 'oneself'.

Ātma-vidyā: Self-knowledge.

Āvaraṇa: A veil. *Ātman* manifesting itself as the world results in not seeing *ātmā* as real, but in seeing the manifestations as real. It is as if *ātmā,* because of its own *māyā* (see), puts a veil on itself resulting in seeing the unreal as real. This veiling power of *māyā* is called *āvaraṇa*.

Avidyā: Nescience or ignorance. That because of which the unreal is taken as the real, and the real as the unreal. The root-cause of illusions and sufferings.

Bandha: The bondage from which one intends to attain liberation.

Bhāna: Any apparent manifest form of consciousness. Literally, 'lustrous appearance'.

Bhānāśraya: The basis of *bhāna* (see).

Bhāva: Any transient form the eternal Reality (*sat*) assumes. Without a *bhāva, sat* never exists, neither can any *bhāva* be there without *sat* existing.

Bhayam: Fear.

Bhoktā (*Bhoktṛ*): Enjoyer; the subject who enjoys.

Bhūmi: Another name for the Earth.

Brahman: The Absolute. Derived from the verb root *bṛh*, 'to grow constantly'. Literally, 'that which grows constantly'.

Brahma-vidyā: The science of the Absolute. Another name for Vedānta.

Cit: Literally, 'consciousness'. The essential content of the imperishable Reality pervading all the perishable and visible forms is pure Consciousness. Hence, *Brahman* is designated as *cit*. See *sat* and *ānanda* also.

Darśana: Literally, 'vision'. The Indian equivalent to 'philosophy'. Vision of Reality as seen from the point of view of a given system of philosophy. Nyāya, Vaiśeṣika, Sāṁkhya, Yoga, Pūrva-Mīmāṁsā and Uttara-Mīmāṁsā are the six such systems of Indian philosophy. Narayana Guru, in his *Darśana-Mālā,* uses this word to mean any particular point of view of the non-dual Reality. He presents ten such visions strung together systematically.

Deva (*Devas*): Gods. Inhabitants of Vedic heaven.

Dharma: Derived from the root *dhṛ*, 'to support'. The universal functional system that sustains the world and life. Righteous way of life fully in harmony with the universal order.

Dharma-śāstra: Scriptures of moral instruction.

Dṛk: Eye. The viewing person, the knowing personal consciousness.

Dṛśya: The visible, objective world; any object of knowledge.

Guṇas: Qualities or functional peculiarities inherent in nature. They are three: *sattva, rajas* and *tamas.*

Guru: (from *gu*, darkness, and *ru,* to counteract). The banisher of darkness or ignorance. A spiritual teacher or preceptor.

Guru-śiṣya-pārasparya: The intimate bipolar rapport between master and disciple. No effective imparting of wisdom is possible in the absence of this rapport.

Idam: This. Stands for 'this world', the world here and now.

Iham: 'This world' as opposed to 'the other world' (*param*).

Jāgaritam: The waking state of consciousness.

Jagat: The world. Literally, 'that which is always on the move'.

Jāti: The social phenomenon of casteism in India. Literally, 'genus'.

Jīva: The Sanskrit equivalent to living organism. Mistaken for the Sanskrit equivalent to 'soul'. Often confused with *ātman*, the Self.

Jīvātmā (*Jīvātman*): Individuated self, as against the universal self (*paramātman*), in Śaṅkara's school of Vedānta.

Jñāna: Wisdom. In the Vedāntic context, the Wisdom of the non-difference of oneself from the universal Reality. The way of *jñāna* (*jñāna-mārga*) is contrasted with that of rituals and actions (*karma-mārga*).

Jñānin: One who possesses *jñāna*. One who has attained elightenment. *Jñāna* means wisdom as contrasted with *karma* (works or rituals). *Jñāna-mārga* or the way of wisdom gives primacy to reason and intuition.

Jñātṛ (*Jñātā*): The knower. Subject in the context of knowing.

Kāraṇa: Cause. Gold is cause and ornament is effect. What really exists in all ornament-forms is gold alone. Similarly, what really exists in the world is *Brahman* alone, which is its cause. This way of thinking is called *sat-kāraṇa-vāda* (theory giving primacy to cause). Indians distinguish two kinds of causes, viz., *upādāna-kāraṇa* (meterial cause) like clay for pots, and *nimitta-kāraṇa* (efficient cause) like the potter and his tools.

Karma: All actions in general. Philosophically the creative urge inherent in the Imperishable Reality, causing the emergence of all manifest forms. In the Vedic context, the ritual of burnt sacrifice enjoined by the Vedas. As a religious belief of Hindus, the incipient memory factors clinging to souls as a result of their deeds in previous births. All are bound to enjoy or suffer the fruits of their deeds, and will have to reincarnate for this purpose. One might be accumulating more *karma*s in the new birth. The vicious chain of *karma*s goes on till one attains final release. Such *karma*s are divided into three categories — *sañcita-karma* (the actions accumulated in all the previous births), *āgāmi-karma* (fresh action to be done in the present life-time), and *prārabdha-karma* (actions already initiated but the eating of their fruits is not finished with).

Karma-phala: The end result of any action or *karma* (see).

Karma-yoga: The *yoga* of action. Realising one's oneness with the total existence by performing deeds with the awareness that all actions belong to total nature, not to any individual being.

Karma yogin: One who lives with the perception of sublimating all one's actions as *karma-yoga* (see).

Kartā (*Kartṛ*): The doer of *karmas*.

Kartṛtva: The state of being the doer of actions.

Krama sṛṣti: The theory that the creation of the world happened as a gradual process. (see *yugapat sṛṣti*).

Lokam: The world. Literally, 'that which is perceptible'.

Matam: Religion. Literally 'one's confirmed opinion'.

Māyā: The mysterious urge inherent in the Absolute (*Brahman* or *ātman*) to unfold itself as all the worlds and the phenomenon of life. The very appearing of the world caused thus ends up in becoming a sort of veil put over the Absolute (see *āvaraṇa*), hiding its vision from our view and making the illusory vision that the apparrent world is the real.

Mokṣa: Final libaration. Literally, 'freedom'. Also called *mukti*.

Mumukṣutva (*Mumukṣutā*): The state of being a restless aspirant for liberation through wisdom.

Nāma: Name. *Nāma* with *rūpa* (form) distinguishes every individual entity in this world.

Naraka: Hell.

Nimitta kāraṇa: Efficient cause.

Nirupādhika jñāna: Unconditioned knowledge. Knowledge not conditioned by subject and object. Knowledge so conditioned is called *sopādhika jñāna*.

Nirveda: Another word for *vairāgya* (see).

Nitya-anitya-viveka: Ability to discriminate the eternal from the transient.

Pāpa: Sin acquired through evil deeds.

Para-Brahman: The higher *Brahman*. Śaṅkara conceives of two aspects of *Brahman*. The lower *Brahman* (*apara-Brahman*) is the ultimate

Reality having the form of the world for its attributes. The higher *Brahman* is attributeless, and hence inconceivable.

Param: The Supreme, the Transcendental. An epithet of *Brahman*.

Paramātman: The Supreme or Transcendental Self. See *Jīvātman*.

Paramānanda: Supreme Happiness.

Parā-māyā: According to Narayana Guru, that aspect of *māyā* because of which the subtle factors such as sense organs and mental faculties get formed in the one Absolute that is Consciousness in essence (see *aparā-māyā*).

Pradhāṇam: That aspect of *māyā*, according to Narayana Guru, because of which the potential for the unfoldment of the world is contained in *Brahman*, just as a tree in a seed.

Prakṛti: Nature. Literally, 'that which is always in an active state'. This activeness is inherent in the ultimate Reality or *Brahman*. *Brahman* in its active state is called *prakṛti*.

Pramāṇas: Any valid means of certitude (*pramā*). Six of them are acceptable to Vedāntins, and their validity, excepting that of *śabda*, is only in worldly knowledge. They are *pratyakṣa* (perception), *anumāna* (inference), *upamāna* (comparison or analogy), *śabda* (scriptures), *arthāpatti* (presumption) and *anupalabdhi* (non-apprehension).

Prapañca: The phenomenal world.

Prapañca-pravāha: A special word coined by Narayana Guru to denote what is called 'eternal flux' in philosophy.

Prārabdha-karma: (see *Karma*).

Pṛthivī: Earth. One of the five basic elements of Nature.

Puṇya: Merit as against *pāpa* (sin).

Purāṇa: Literally, 'the ancient'. The collection of legends of antiquity, meant mainly for teaching the common man, the philosophy of the Upaniṣads with the help of numerous tales.

Pūrṇa: That which is complete in all respects.

Pūrva-pakṣa: In the context of a philosophical argument, the one who opposes the proponent of any particular theory. In wisdom-dialogues, a disciple who raises genuine doubts before a Guru.

Rajas: The active modality of Nature (see *guṇas*).

Rasa: Essence; juice; aesthetic feeling.

Rūpa: Form, along with *nāma* (name), distinguishes every individual entity in this world. Hence the world is often spoken of as constituted of *nāma* and *rūpa*.

Saccidānanda (*sat+cit+ānanda*): Existence-consciousness-value-experience; the only positive definition of *Brahman*. See *sat*, *cit*, and *ānanda*.

Sādhanā: Spiritual discipline undergone for the attainment of a particular goal (*sidhhi*).

Sama: One of the two modes in which human consciousness functions, in which one Reality alone is perceived in all the multiple apparent forms.

Śama: Checking the mind and turning it away from distractions. One of the six qualities to be developed by self-effort as part of spiritual discipline. The other five are *dama* (self-restraint by withdrawing sense-organs from their objects), *uparati* (non-dependence on the external), *titikṣā* (endurance), *śraddhā* (full faith in the words of one's *guru* and of the scriptures), and *samādhāna* (having the thought of *Brahman* always in mind).

Śamādi-ṣatka-sampatti: The six disciplines self-imposed by a genuine seekeer (see *Śama*).

Sāmānya: The generic.

Samvit: Another word for *cit*. Pure, Unconditioned Consciousness.

Sañcita-karma: See *Karma*.

Sapta-jihvā: A name of fire. Literally, 'the seven-tongued'.

Śarīra: Literally 'that which perishes'. The physical body or the visible form.

Sat: That which exists always. The subsisting reality in all the transistory forms of the visible world, even as gold is the subsisting reality in all ornaments. *Brahman*, as this subsisting Reality, is designated as *sat*. See *ānanda* and *cit* also.

Sattva: One of the triple modalities of Nature, originally conceived by Kapila in the *Sāṁkhya-Pravacana-Sūtras* (see *Guṇa*s).

Sāyujya: Experiencing one's own merger in the being of the total.

Śiṣya: A disciple; seeker.

Smṛti: Learning or scriptural lore remembered by a student when he applies wisdom-teaching in his practical life. Obligatory conduct and religious duties belong to this category. Also known as *Dharma-Śāstra*. What is taught by them are subject to change in accordance with time and clime.

Sopādhika-jñāna: Knowledge conditioned by subject and object as against *nirupādhika-jñāna*.

Śraddhā: One of the prerequisites on the part of a seeker. Willingness to have full faith in the truthfulness of the word of the *guru* and of the scriptures. A necessary stepping stone to *manana*.

Suṣupti: The deep sleep state of mind.

Svapna: The dreaming state of mind.

Svarga: The Vedic heaven or paradise inhabited by *deva*s (gods) whose chief is Indra.

Tamas: Dark and inert (see *Guṇa*s).

Tapas: Austere self-discipline. Literally, 'heating up'.

Titikṣā: Endurance of troubles incidental in life, without petulance or self-pity. One of the prerequisite qualities of a seeker.

Tripuṭi: Three aspects involved in the event of knowing something; namely, the knower, the known and the act of a knowing. Literally, 'the three-petalled'.

Turīya: Literally 'the fourth'. The transcendal state of consciousness in which the *tripuṭi* merges in the all engulfing self-radiance.

Narayana Guru defines it as, 'to know that which is bottomless and topless, from top of bottom'.

Upādāna-karaṇa: See *Kāraṇa*.

Upādhi: Conditioning factors that make indistinct Reality appear in distinct forms.

Uparati: The disposition of not being influenced by external matters in deciding what to do and how to do in the course of life.

Vairāgya: Sense of detachment towards everything transient.

Varṇa: Literally, 'colour'. The four different psychological types recognised by traditional Indian psychologists. They are, brāhmaṇa, kṣatriya, vaiśya and śūdra. It was confused with *jāti* (see), making it instrumental for social discrimination and exploitation of the downtrodden.

Vāsanā: Incipient memory factors and inborn traits in individuals. Such unconscious factors decide to a great extent how one behaves in life.

Vāyu: Air. The god of air.

Veda: The earliest of the Indian scriptures, collected into four volumes, namely the *R̥gveda, Yajurveda, Sāmaveda* and *Atharvaveda*. They praise gods like Indra, Varuṇa, Mitra and other phenomenal gods of nature. They were later overcome by the Upaniṣads. The word *veda* means 'knowledge'. The Vedas generally stand for rituals (*karma*).

Vedānta: When the Vedic teaching was revalued in philosophical terms by later *r̥ṣis*, a body of literature called Vedānta arose in the history of Indian thought. This often goes contrary to the Vedic tendency of rituals and obligations, announcing freedom and stressing self-realisation. Latter we find Śaṅkara, Rāmānuja and Madhva, referred to as three typical Vedāntic philosophers, although the *gurus* of the Vedāntic line (*paramparā*) are many.

Vidyā: Knowledge. That function of consciousness because of which one understands the Real as the real and unreal as the unreal.

Viśeṣa: The specific (see *Sāmānya*).

Viśeṣa-jñāna: Any knowledge one acquires about anything specific.

Vivarta: Illusory appearance. Denoting the process by which an effect appears in a cause without the latter undergoing any intrinsic change, e.g., the appearance of waves in ocean.

Vṛtti: Organic function, whether bodily or mental.

Yoga: (From the root *yuj*, 'to join') Each finding one's inseparable oneness with the one causal Reality, just as an ornament finds its oneness with gold. As a contemplative method of self-enquiry, the way of expressing an inexpressible reality by showing its two opposite sides and leaving the unitive meaning to be understood by the reader or seeker on his own. For example, attaining immortality and crossing over death are two expressions meaning the same. But these two expressions are opposite in nature. They have in between them a meaning that cannot be expressed as it is.

Different systems of *Yoga* have been developed in India, each giving emphasis to some particular pair to be joined together. Patañjali's system is known also as *Rāja-Yoga*. The names *Haṭha-Yoga, Karma-Yoga, Jñāna-Yoga, Bhakti-Yoga*, are popular. Each of the eighteen chapters of the *Bhagavad Gītā* is also named a *Yoga*. The *Bhagavad Gītā* itself claims to be a *Yoga-Śāstra* (textbook on the science of *yoga*).

Yoga-buddhi: The awareness attained by the method of *Yoga* (See *yoga*).

Yogī (*Yogin*): One who is adept in *Yoga*.

Bibliography

Bergson, Henry, *Creative Evolution* (University Press of America, 1983).

Bergson, Henri, *The Two Sources of Morality and Religion* (University of Notre Dam Press Indiana, 1977).

Bhaskaran, Dr. T., *Sree Narayana Guruvinte Sampurna Kritikal* (Malayalam) (The complete works of Narayana Guru with commentary) (Mathrubhoomi Publications, Calicut, 1985).

Capra, Fritjof, *The Tao of Physics* (Fantana Paperbacks Glasgow, 1988).

Chakravarti, V.R. Srisaila, *The Philosophy of Ramanuja* (V.R.S. Chakravarti, Madras, 1974).

Guru, Narayana, *Sampoorna Kritikal* (Malayalam), (Narayana Gurukula, Varkala, Trivandrum, 2002).

Guru, Nataraja, *The Bhagavad Gita* (Narayana Gurukula, Varkala, Trivandrum, 1989).

———, *An Integrated Science of the Absolute* (D.K. Printworld, New Delhi, 2001).

———, *One Hundred Verses of Self-Instruction* (Narayana Gurukula, Varkala, Trivandrum, 1970).

———, *The Philosophy of A Guru* (Narayana Gurukula, Varkala Trivandrum, 1986).

———, *The Search for a Norm in Western Thought* (Narayana Gurukula, Varkala, Trivandrum, 1986).

———, *Vedanta Revalued and Restated* (Narayana Gurukula, Varkala, Trivandrum, 1987).

———, *The Word of the Guru* (Narayana Gurukula, Varkala, Trivandrum, 1952).

———, *Wisdom* (D.K. Printworld, New Delhi, 1995).

Murchie, Guy, *The Seven Mysteries of Life* (Houghton Mifflin Co., Boston, 1981).

Omana, Dr. S., *The Philosophy of Sree Narayana Guru* (Narayana Gurukula, Varkala, Trivandrum, 1984).

Plato, *The Republic* (Random H...

Prasad, Swami Muni Narayana, ... *...nisad* (D.K. Printworld, New Delhi, 2000).

———, *Chandogya Upaniṣad* (Unpublished).

———, *Kaṭha Upaniṣad* (D.K. Printworld, New Delhi, 1998).

———, *Kena Upaniṣad* (D.K. Printworld, New Delhi, 1994).

———, *Muṇḍaka Upaniṣad* (D.K. Printworld, New Delhi, 1998).

———, *Praśna Upaniṣad* (D.K. Printworld, New Delhi, 1998).

———, *Vedānta Sūtras of Narayana Guru* (D.K. Printworld, New Delhi, 2003).

———, *Vedānta up to Narayana Guru* (Unpublished).

Śaṅkarācārya, *Vedānta Sūtras* — Commentary, Translated by George Thibaut, (Motilal Banarsidass, Delhi, 1973).

———, *Vivekacūḍāmaṇi,* Translated by Swami Madhavananda (Advaita Ashram, Calcutta, 1970).

Sharma, Dr. B.N.K., *Philosophy of Sri Madhvacharya* (Bharatiya Vidyabhavan, Bombay, 1962).

Srinivasachari, P.N., *The Philosophy of Viśiṣṭādvaita* (Adayar Library Madras, 1970).

Upaniṣad Saṁgrahaḥ (Motilal Banarasidass, Delhi, 1980).

Vidyananda, Swami, *Darśana-mālā*, Commentary (Malayalam) (Sivagiri Mutt, Varkala, Trivandrum, 1976).

Yati, Nitya Chaitanya, *Epistemology of Gnosis* (Narayana Gurukula, Varkala, Trivandrum, 1985).

———, *Neither This Nor That . . . But AUṀ* (D.K. Printworld, New Delhi, 1995).

———, *The Psychology of Darsanamala* (Narayana Gurukula, Varkala, Trivandrum, 1987).

Zukav, Gary, *The Dancing Wu Li Masters* (Fontana Paperbacks, Glasgow, 1989).

Index